Editorial Project Manager
Eric Migliaccio

Editor in Chief
Karen J. Goldfluss, M.S. Ed.

Creative Director
Sarah M. Fournier

Cover Artist
Diem Pascarella

Illustrator
Mark Mason

Art Coordinator
Renée Mc Elwee

Imaging
Amanda R. Harter

Publisher
Mary D. Smith, M.S. Ed.

MASTERING COM

TCR 8060

Using Mu
Reading Sources

MW00380473

Includes:

- 22 Units with 3 – 5 related text sources in a variety of genres and formats

- Multiple question types that promote higher-order thinking skills

- Open-ended response opportunities to encourage close reading

- Correlated to the Common Core State Standards

Teacher Created Resources

Author
Karen McRae

CORRELATED TO COMMON CORE STANDARDS

For correlations to the Common Core State Standards, see pages 109–112 of this book or visit *http://www.teachercreated.com/standards/*.

Teacher Created Resources
6421 Industry Way
Westminster, CA 92683
www.teachercreated.com

ISBN: 978-1-4206-8060-7

© 2015 Teacher Created Resources
Made in U.S.A.

Teacher Created Resources

Table of Contents

Introduction

Here we are, teaching and learning at the beginning of a new era of educational standards: the Common Core Era. This new directive has ushered in a slew of educational guidelines that are somewhat familiar and yet entirely ambitious. While the Common Core State Standards for English Language Arts address many educational basics (reading comprehension, proficiency in the conventions of English grammar, the ability to express oneself both in writing and in speech), they also seek to define what it means to be a literate, resourceful, perceptive person in the 21st century. Ultimately, they aim to equip each student with the tools needed to be that kind of person.

With this new, ambitious focus comes the need for a new type of educational material—one that challenges and interests students while meeting the multifaceted criteria of the Common Core. There are a total of 22 units in *Mastering Complex Text Using Multiple Reading Sources*, and each one fits the bill.

Introduction *(cont.)*

✳ The units in this book are both familiar and innovative.

They are familiar in that they pair reading passages with activities that test reading comprehension. They are innovative in how they accomplish this goal through the use of multiple text sources and multiple answer formats. These materials promote deeper understanding and thought processes by prompting students to analyze, synthesize, hypothesize, and empathize.

✳ The use of multiple reading sources promotes close reading.

Close reading is the underlying goal of the Common Core State Standards for English Language Arts. Close reading involves understanding not just the explicit content of a reading passage but also all of the nuances contained therein. A close reading of a text reveals all of the inferential and structural components of the content, while also illuminating the craft that went into the writing of it.

The Common Core State Standards suggest that the best way to foster close reading of informational text is through text complexity. It offers four factors needed to create a high level of text complexity—all four of which are achieved through this book's use of multiple reading sources:

Factor	Meaning
1. Levels of Purpose	The purpose of the text should be implicit, hidden, or obscured in some way.
2. Structure	Texts of high complexity tend to have complex, implicit, or unconventional structures.
3. Language Conventionality or Clarity	Texts should use domain-specific language and feature language that is figurative, ironic, ambiguous, or otherwise unfamiliar.
4. Knowledge Demands	Complex texts make assumptions that readers can use life experiences, cultural awareness, and content knowledge to supplement their understanding of a text.

✳ The activities prompt students to explore the reading material from all angles.

By completing the four different activities found in each unit, students will be able to display a broad understanding of the reading material. Each activity and question is designed to make students think about what they have read—everything from how it was written, to why it was written that way, to how its subject matter can be applied to their lives. They gain experience locating information, making inferences from it, and applying knowledge in a variety of ways.

The units in this book are supplemented by a comprehensive answer key (pages 101–108) and a full list of Common Core State Standards correlations (pages 109–112). And even more educational value can be mined from each unit's reading material with "Additional Activities" (page 100). Make copies of this page (one per student per unit) and have students follow the instructions.

How to Use This Book

This book is divided into 22 units, which do not need to be taught in any particular order. Each unit is composed of reading material (one or two pages) and activity pages (two or three pages):

Reading Material

The reading material for each unit consists of three or four text sources. Have students read all of a unit's text sources before proceeding to the activity pages. These sources complement each other, and a connective thread (or threads) runs throughout them. Sometimes these connections will be explicit, while at other times they will be hidden or obscured.

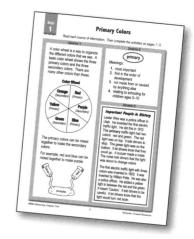

> ✳ **Another Approach** After reading the source material, ask students to name all of the ways in which the reading sources seem to be related or connected. See page 100 for more details.

Activity Pages

Each unit is supported by two or three pages of activities. These activity pages are divided into four parts:

Part 1

One recurring theme in the Common Core's Informational Text strand is that students should be able to draw information from multiple print sources and demonstrate the ability to locate an answer to a question quickly. This section directly correlates to that standard. Students will gain valuable practice in scanning multiple text sources in order to locate information.

Before beginning this section, remind students to read the directions carefully. Some of the information can be found in two or more sources, which means that students will need to fill in more than one bubble in those instances.

> ✳ **Another Approach** Have your students practice their recognition of genres and formats. For each unit, have them fill in the chart on page 100.

Part 2

In this section, students are asked to provide the best answer(s) to multiple-choice questions. What sets these apart from the usual multiple-choice questions is their emphasis on higher-order thinking skills. Very few questions ask for simple recall of information. Instead, these questions are designed to provide practice and strengthen knowledge in a variety of areas, including the following:

✳ inference	✳ word etymology	✳ compare and contrast
✳ deduction	✳ parts of speech	✳ cause and effect
✳ grammar and usage	✳ literary devices	✳ analogies
✳ vocabulary in context	✳ authorial intent	✳ computation

> ✳ **Another Approach** Ask each student to write an original multiple-choice question based on the reading sources. Use the best or most interesting questions to create a student-generated quiz. See page 100 for more details.

How to Use This Book *(cont.)*

Activity Pages *(cont.)*

Part 3

This section takes the skills addressed in Part 1 and approaches them from another angle. Part 3 is in the form of a scavenger hunt that asks students to search the sources in order to locate a word or phrase that fits the criteria described.

> ✳ **Another Approach** Assign students to small groups, and have each group collaboratively come up with a suitable scavenger hunt from the reading material. These student-created scavenger hunts can then be completed and discussed by the entire class. See page 100 for more details.

Part 4

This section is composed of three questions that ask students to integrate information from several texts on the same topic in order to write knowledgeably about a subject. The vast majority of these questions are open-ended, while the rest involve using a new format (e.g., chart, diagram, graph) to organize and/or interpret data and information.

The questions in this section challenge students to blend close-reading concepts with flexible-thinking skills. Students are asked to do the following:

Analyze	Synthesize	Hypothesize	Empathize
✳ authorial choices ✳ intent of characters/ historical figures ✳ overall meanings ✳ quotations in context ✳ statistical data	✳ combine different takes on the same subject ✳ use information from different genres and formats (nonfiction, fiction, graphs, etc.) to draw conclusions ✳ compare and contrast characters, ideas, and concepts ✳ draw conclusions from information and/or numerical data	✳ make predictions about future events ✳ explore alternatives to previous choices	✳ connect to one's own life ✳ put oneself in a character's/ historical figure's place

> ✳ **Another Approach** The Common Core places a strong emphasis on teaching and applying speaking and listening skills. Many of the questions in Part 4 lend themselves well to meeting standards from this strand. Have individual students present oral reports on specific Part 4 questions. Or, form groups of students and ask them to engage in collaborative discussion before presenting their findings.

Primary Colors

Read each source of information. Then complete the activities on pages 7–9.

Source 1

A color wheel is a way to organize the different colors that we see. A basic color wheel shows the three primary colors and the three secondary colors. There are many colors other than these.

Color Wheel

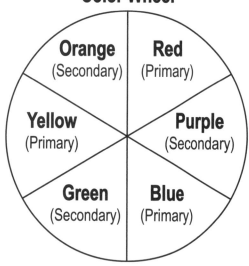

The primary colors can be mixed together to make the secondary colors.

For example, red and blue can be mixed together to make purple.

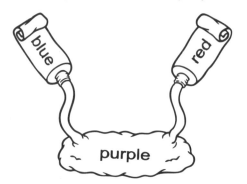

Source 2

primary

Meanings:

1. most important
2. first in the order of development
3. not made from or caused by anything else
4. relating to schooling for children ages 5–10

Source 3

Important People in History

Lester Wire was a police officer in Utah. He invented the first electric traffic light. He did this in 1912. This **primary** traffic light had two colors: red and green. The red light was on top. It told drivers to stop. The green light was on the bottom. It let drivers know that they could go. A buzzer made a noise. The noise told drivers that the light was about to change colors.

The first electric traffic light with three colors was invented in 1920. It was invented by William Potts. He was also a police officer. He added a yellow light in between the red and the green. It meant 'Caution.' It told drivers to be careful. It let drivers know that the light would turn red soon.

Primary Colors *(cont.)*

Name: _____

Part 1: Read each idea. Which source gives you this information? Fill in the correct bubble for each source.

Information	Sources ➡	1	2	3
1. Yellow is a primary color.		○	○	○
2. Yellow was added to traffic lights in 1920.		○	○	○
3. A police officer invented the first electric traffic light.		○	○	○

Part 2: Fill in the bubble next to the best answer to each question.

4. What could be used in place of the word *caution*?

Ⓐ Be careful.   Ⓒ Go now.

Ⓑ Stop now.   Ⓓ Driving is primary.

5. How was Lester Wire's traffic light *primary*?

Ⓐ It was the most important traffic light.

Ⓑ It was the first traffic light of its kind.

Ⓒ It was not made from anything else.

Ⓓ It made loud noises.

6. Which of these things would be *secondary*?

Ⓐ the most important thing

Ⓑ the second most important thing

Ⓒ the least important thing

Ⓓ all things

Part 3: Search <u>Source 2</u> of "Primary Colors" to find the following:

7. a word that means "education" or "learning" _____

Primary Colors *(cont.)*

Name: _____

Part 4: Use the sources to answer the following questions.

8. Look at the traffic light below. For each circle, follow these steps:

▶ On Line 1, write the color name.

▶ On Line 2, tell what kind of color it is. Write **primary** or **secondary**.

▶ On Line 3, write what the light means. Write **stop**, **go**, or **caution**.

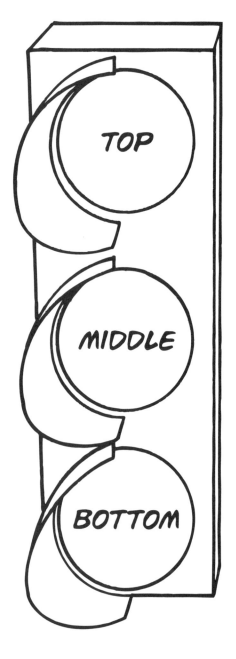

Top Light

Line 1: _____

Line 2: _____

Line 3: _____

Middle Light

Line 1: _____

Line 2: _____

Line 3: _____

Bottom Light

Line 1: _____

Line 2: _____

Line 3: _____

Name: _____

9. Look again at Source 2. Which meaning best explains why red, yellow, and blue are called primary colors? Write this meaning in the box.

[ ]

Then explain your answer.

_____

_____

_____

10. The first traffic light only had two colors. It also had a buzzer.

   A. Do you think it was a good idea to add the color yellow to traffic lights? Explain.

_____

_____

_____

   B. For today's drivers, which would be more helpful: a yellow light or a buzzer? Explain.

_____

_____

_____

Buzz Words

Read each source below and on page 11. Then complete the activities on pages 12–13.

Source 1

Mr. Hill said, "Does anybody have a science question? For the next 10 minutes, you can ask any question you want about science. What are you curious to know?"

Nick raised his hand, "Why do bees buzz?"

"Great question," said Mr. Hill. "A flying insect has wings. Its flapping wings push against the air. This helps the insect stay up in the air. The smaller the wings, the more times they must flap to keep the insect up. Bees have small wings. Their wings must flap about 200 times every second. All of that flapping makes a sound. The sound it makes is "bzzz." Other insects also flap their wings. A mosquito's wings are even smaller than a bee's. It must flap its wings about 400 times per second. It makes a whining sound. A butterfly has bigger wings. It only has to flap its wings about six times every second. A butterfly is not very loud. Its wings aren't pushing against the air nearly as much as a bee's or a mosquito's wings."

Source 2

Mr. Achoo asked his students, "What sound does a car horn make?"

His students said, "Honk!"

Mr. Achoo asked his students, "What sound does a bee make?"

His students said, "Bzzz!"

Mr. Achoo asked his students, "What sound does a dog make?"

Vera said, "Ruff!" Victor said, "Grrr!" Violet said, "Yip!" Wally said, "Woof!"

Mr. Achoo asked his students, "What do we call words like *honk*, *bzzz*, and *ruff*?"

None of the students said a word.

Mr. Achoo said, "Words like *honk*, *bzzz*, *ruff*, and *woof* name the sounds we hear all around us. We call these words *onomatopoeia*. What a long, fancy word! Here is how we pronounce this long, fancy word: **ahh-no-mah-toe-pee-uh**. What a nice sound that word has! Any word that sounds like the sound something makes is an onomatopoeia."

Source 3

Bzzz. Do you think of bees or other insects when you hear that sound? Many people don't like bees. Bees buzz, and they also sting. That is why many people don't like the *bzzz* sound. How about you?

I like the *bzzz* sound. It calms me. Maybe that is why I became a beekeeper. I keep bees and help take care of their hives. I do this so I can collect honey. I am not too afraid of bees. I am careful, though. I know that a bee sting can be painful. It also can be dangerous.

I wear special clothes to protect me. I wear a helmet to protect my head. I wear a veil to protect my face and neck. A veil is made of wire mesh. Mesh has tiny holes in it. This lets me breathe through the mesh. I can see through it, but the bees can't get in. It is most important to protect my face and neck from bee stings.

My white suit has long sleeves. My light-colored pants are long. I wear light colors because I don't want the bees to fear me. If they fear me, they might sting me. I don't want to look like one of their enemies. Their enemies are dark. Their enemies are bears, skunks, raccoons, and other animals.

I also wear boots. I tape my boots to my pants. If I don't, a bee could get inside. I'm not too afraid of bees, but I don't want to feel one crawling up my leg!

Buzz Words *(cont.)*

Part 1: Read each idea. Which source gives you this information? Fill in the correct bubble for each source. (Note: More than one bubble may be filled in for each idea.)

Information	Sources ➡	1	2	3
1. Bees are insects.		○	○	○
2. Bees make a "bzzz" sound.		○	○	○
3. Bears are the enemies of bees.		○	○	○

Part 2: Fill in the bubble next to the best answer to each question.

4. Which of these statements is **not** true about a bee's wings?

Ⓐ They flap twice as fast as a mosquito's wings.

Ⓑ They flap half as fast as a mosquito's wings.

Ⓒ They are smaller than a butterfly's wings.

Ⓓ They make noise when they flap.

5. Which shows the correct order, **from slow to fast**, of how these insects flap their wings?

Ⓐ butterfly, mosquito, bee

Ⓑ butterfly, bee, mosquito

Ⓒ mosquito, bee, butterfly

Ⓓ bee, mosquito, butterly

6. Look at the teacher's name in Source 2. What does his name most sound like?

Ⓐ a bee buzzing

Ⓑ a person snoring

Ⓒ a car horn honking

Ⓓ a person sneezing

Part 3: Search <u>Source 3</u> of "Buzz Words" to find the following:

7. a word that means the opposite of "friends" _____

Name: _____

Part 4: Use the sources to answer the following questions.

8. Your friend is going to watch a baseball game outdoors. She is worried that a bee will land on her and sting her. Tell her what would be the best color to wear to keep this from happening. Explain the reason for your answer.

_____

_____

_____

9. Look at the picture to the right. Find the arrow. To what piece of clothing does it point?

_____

Find the sentence in Source 3 that gives you this information. Write that sentence here:

_____

_____

_____

10. Look at the sentences below. Circle each onomatopoeia word.

I walked through the flower patch at the edge of the woods. A calm breeze

whirred through the leaves of the oak trees. A bird chirped in one tree.

Another bird squawked as it flew over my head.

Star Light, Star Bright

Read each source of information. Then complete the activities on pages 15–17.

Source 1

The stars in the sky look like they twinkle. They also look very small. The truth is that the stars in the sky are very big, and they do not twinkle at all.

Stars are huge. Many are bigger than Earth! They look small because they are so far away. We can only see them because they are so big and bright. The brightest star in the night sky is called Sirius. It is also known as the "Dog Star."

The light from stars has to travel far to get to Earth. There is a lot of stuff between us and those stars. There is a lot of air. This air is always moving. We are seeing the stars through this moving air. It makes the stars look as though they are twinkling. If you could get much closer to the stars, you would see that they do not twinkle at all.

Source 2

constellation

Meaning: a group of stars that form a pattern in the night sky

Example:

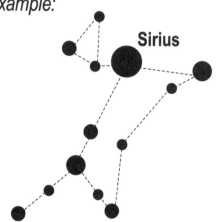

There are many constellations. The one above is called Canis Major*. "Canis Major" means "big dog" in the Latin language. Sirius is one star in Canis Major. Sirius is the brightest star in the night sky.

* Canis Major is made up of more stars than are shown in the picture.

Source 3

Tim and his dad were looking at the night sky. They were looking at the stars. Tim's dad asked, "Do you see that really bright star?"

Tim saw it. "Yes," he said. "I think that star is the brightest one in the sky."

"It is," said Tim's dad. "That star is called Sirius. People also call it the Dog Star."

"Why is it called that?" asked Tim.

Star Light, Star Bright *(cont.)*

Name: _____

Part 1: Read each idea. Which source gives you this information? Fill in the correct bubble for each source. (Note: More than one bubble may be filled in for each idea.)

Information	Sources ➡	1	2	3
1. There is a constellation called Canis Major.		○	○	○
2. There is a star named Sirius.		○	○	○
3. Sirius is called the "Dog Star."		○	○	○

Part 2: Fill in the bubble next to the best answer to each question.

4. Which one of these statements is true about **all** stars?

  Ⓐ They are small, and they twinkle.

  Ⓑ Their names mean "greater dog."

  Ⓒ Their light must travel far to get to Earth.

  Ⓓ They are all a part of one constellation.

5. What is the **main topic** of Source 1?

  Ⓐ Stars are big and bright.

  Ⓑ Stars are bigger than Earth.

  Ⓒ Sirius is the brightest star in the sky.

  Ⓓ Stars do not really twinkle.

6. In the Latin language, the word "major" means "big." What must the word "canis" mean?

  Ⓐ Sirius   Ⓒ dog

  Ⓑ star   Ⓓ twinkle

Part 3: Search <u>Source 1</u> of "Star Light, Star Bright" to find the following:

7. a word that rhymes with "birth" and "worth" _____

Star Light, Star Bright *(cont.)*

Name: _____

Part 4: Use the sources to answer the following questions.

8. Imagine you are standing outside. It is nighttime. You are looking at a light shining far away. Would the light be more likely to look like it is twinkling on a very windy night or on a night with no wind? Explain your answer. Tell which source gave you this answer.

_____

_____

_____

_____

_____

9. Tim asks his dad a question. Give Tim an answer. Write the next lines in the story. Take your best guess based on what you have learned in the sources.

"Why is Sirius called the 'Dog Star'?" asked Tim.

Tim's dad said, " _____

_____

_____

_____

_____

_____

_____."

Star Light, Star Bright *(cont.)*

Name: _____

Part 4 *(cont.)*:

10. Look at the picture below.

    A. First, connect the dots in order from 1–14.

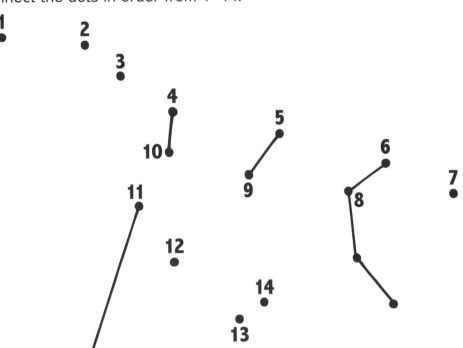

This constellation is called Ursa Major. In Latin, the word "ursa" means "bear."

    B. What does "Ursa Major" mean in English? _____

    C. Do you think this is a good name for this constellation? Why or why not?

_____

_____

    D. If you had to give this constellation a different name, what would you call it?

_____

Why? _____

_____

Award-Winning Cookies

Read each source below and on page 19. Then complete the activities on pages 20–21.

Source 1

Aunt Patty's Peanut Butter Cookies

Ingredients

- 2 cups peanut butter
- $1\frac{1}{2}$ cups sugar
- 2 eggs
- 2 teaspoons baking soda
- 1 teaspoon vanilla extract
- $\frac{1}{2}$ cup chocolate chips

Source 2

I will be the contest winner this year. I'm sure of it. I can't lose! I will make award-winning cookies this year.

Last year, I came in second place. This year, I have a better recipe. This year, Aunt Patty is letting me use her recipe. Everybody loves Aunt Patty's peanut butter cookies. I will definitely come in first place this year!

I mix peanut butter and sugar. I blend these two ingredients until they are smooth. Then I mix in one egg. Once that is mixed in, I add in one more egg. Then I mix in two tablespoons of baking soda, a teaspoon of vanilla, and $\frac{1}{2}$ cup of chocolate chips. The dough smells great! I can't taste the dough because it's not safe to eat raw eggs.

Pure
Baking Soda

I roll the dough into little balls. I put these dough balls into a hot oven. They begin to bake. Wonderful smells fill my kitchen. The cookies smell like warm peanut butter. They smell like melting chocolate. The cookies smell like first place.

Source 3

Dear Diary,

I don't understand. What could have gone wrong? I thought I followed Aunt Patty's cookie recipe perfectly. I must not have. My cookies were terrible! They were flat and crumbly. They had a bitter taste. I don't think anyone took more than one bite.

Everybody who enters wins some prize. Those are the rules of the contest. I came in first place this year. I came in first place in the category "Strangest-Tasting Cookie." That was not the award I expected to win.

—Lily

Source 4

Baking Measurements

3 teaspoons = 1 tablespoon

8 tablespoons = $\frac{1}{2}$ cup

16 tablespoons = 1 cup

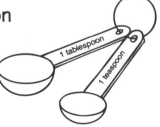

Award-Winning Cookies *(cont.)*

Name: _____

Part 1: Read each idea. Which source gives you this information? Fill in the correct bubble for each source. (Note: More than one bubble may be filled in for each idea.)

Information Sources ➡	1	2	3	4
1. Aunt Patty has a recipe for peanut butter cookies.	○	○	○	○
2. Lily is baking cookies for a contest.	○	○	○	○
3. Lily won second place in last year's contest.	○	○	○	○

Part 2: Fill in the bubble next to the best answer to each question.

4. What is the main reason Lily doesn't taste the dough before she bakes her cookies?

   Ⓐ The cookies will taste better once they are baked.

   Ⓑ It is not safe to eat uncooked cookie dough.

   Ⓒ She wants to save all her cookies for the contest.

   Ⓓ She doesn't have time to taste the cookie dough.

5. Which of these things happened third?

   Ⓐ Lily baked Aunt Patty's cookies.

   Ⓑ Aunt Patty gave Lily her cookie recipe.

   Ⓒ Lily won the prize for "Strangest-Tasting Cookie."

   Ⓓ Lily mixed peanut butter and sugar.

6. What does Lily mean when she says that the cookies "smell like first place"?

   Ⓐ They smell like warm peanut butter.

   Ⓑ They smell like melting chocolate.

   Ⓒ They smell like they are safe to eat.

   Ⓓ They smell good enough to win a contest.

Part 3: Search <u>Source 3</u> of "Award-Winning Cookies" to find the following:

7. a word that rhymes with "tries" _____

Award-Winning Cookies *(cont.)*

Name: _____

Part 4: Use the sources to answer the following questions.

8. How many tablespoons of sugar are used in Aunt Patty's recipe? _____
Explain how you know this answer.

_____

_____

_____

9. Picture someone taking a bite of Lily's peanut butter cookies. What expression is on that person's face? In the box, draw a picture of that person's face. On the lines, describe how that person feels as he or she eats the cookie.

_____

_____

_____

_____

10. Why do Lily's cookies not taste good? What mistake did she make? Use information from the sources to explain your answer.

_____

_____

_____

_____

Many Moons Ago

Read each source below and on page 23. Then complete the activities on pages 24–25.

Source 1

A moon is a large, natural object in space. It orbits (goes around) a larger object in space. Earth has one moon. Our moon orbits Earth. It takes about one month for our moon to do this.

Some other planets have many moons. Some planets do not have any moons.

Source 2

The Sun is the center of our solar system. It gives light and heat. It is the largest object in our solar system.

Our solar system contains eight planets. These eight planets orbit the Sun. They can be divided into two groups: Inner Planets and Outer Planets.

The four planets closest to the Sun are the Inner Planets. These four planets are Mercury, Venus, Earth, and Mars. Mercury and Venus are the closest planets to the Sun. These two planets are very hot. Our planet is the third planet from the Sun. Mars is the fourth planet. There is a lot of space between Mars and the fifth planet. The fifth planet is Jupiter.

Jupiter, Saturn, Uranus, and Neptune are the four Outer Planets. They are very far away and very cold.

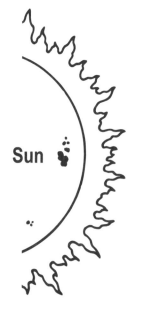 **Sun**   **Mercury**   **Venus**   **Earth**   **Mars**

Unit 5

Many Moons Ago *(cont.)*

Source 3

"many moons ago"

This saying means "a long time ago."

Example: The old man said, "Many moons ago, I was the fastest runner at my school."

Source 4

The charts below show how many moons orbit each planet in our solar system. Some moons have been discovered within the last 10 years. In fact, one of Neptune's moons was discovered in 2013. How do these new moons suddenly appear?

They don't suddenly appear. They have been there all along. We just need newer and better equipment to see them. With new telescopes and spacecraft, we are able to discover moons that are farther and farther away. This means that there may be other moons that we have not yet discovered.

The chart below shows the moons we knew about at two different times: 2004 and 2014.

Planets (in order from the Sun)

	1. Mercury	2. Venus	3. Earth	4. Mars	5. Jupiter	6. Saturn	7. Uranus	8. Neptune
Number of Moons as of January 1, 2004	0	0	1	2	62	32	27	13
Number of Moons as of January 1, 2014	0	0	1	2	67	62	27	14

Name: _____

Part 1: Read each idea. Which source gives you this information? Fill in the correct bubble for each source. (Note: More than one bubble may be filled in for each idea.)

Information Sources ➡	1	2	3	4
1. Earth is the third planet from the Sun.	○	○	○	○
2. Earth is one of the Inner Planets.	○	○	○	○
3. Some planets do not have any moons.	○	○	○	○

Part 2: Fill in the bubble next to the best answer to each question.

4. Which of these things happened "many moons ago"?

   Ⓐ The first telescope was invented.

   Ⓑ Neptune's 14th moon was discovered.

   Ⓒ Our moon last orbited Earth.

   Ⓓ You woke up this morning.

5. The drawing in Source 2 shows the Sun and

   Ⓐ all of the planets in our solar system.

   Ⓑ just the Inner Planets in our solar system.

   Ⓒ just the Outer Planets in our solar system.

   Ⓓ all of the moons in our solar system.

6. Most likely, what is the main reason why the Outer Planets are colder than the Inner Planets?

   Ⓐ because the word "outer" means "colder"

   Ⓑ because they have many more moons

   Ⓒ because they are farther from the Sun

   Ⓓ because they are far from Earth

Part 3: Search <u>Source 1</u> of "Many Moons Ago" to find a word that means the following:

7. the opposite of "artificial" _____

Many Moons Ago *(cont.)*

Name: _____

Part 4: Use the sources to answer the following questions.

11. Complete the paragraph. On each blank line, write either the word **moons** or the word **planets**.

There are eight _____ in our solar system.

Combined, there are over 170 _____ in our

solar system. Many _____ have two or more

_____. Mercury and Venus do not have any

_____.

Many _____ ago, we knew less about our solar

system. With new telescopes and spacecraft, we learn more and more

all of the time.

12. In the year 2006, astronomers used a special new telescope. With this telescope, they discovered nine small moons orbiting one of the planets. Use Source 4 to figure out which planet this must have been. Name the planet. Explain your answer.

_____

_____

_____

13. Source 4 contains moon charts from the years 2004 and 2014. Imagine seeing a moon chart from the year 2024. Why could it be different than the one from 2014?

_____

_____

_____

_____

Supply the Answer

Read each source below and on page 27. Then complete the activities on pages 28–30.

Source 1

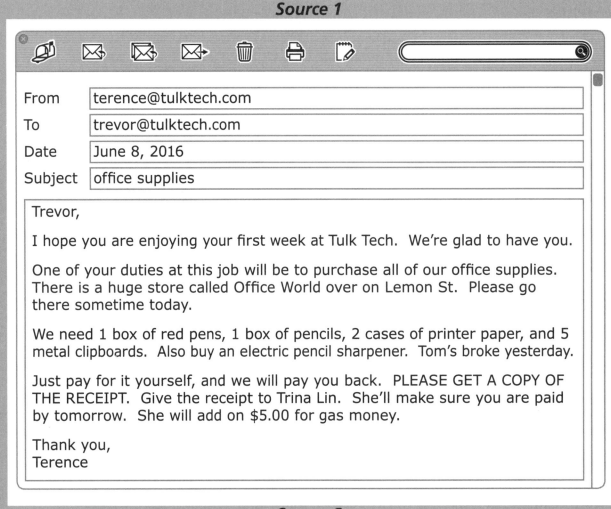

From	terence@tulktech.com
To	trevor@tulktech.com
Date	June 8, 2016
Subject	office supplies

Trevor,

I hope you are enjoying your first week at Tulk Tech. We're glad to have you.

One of your duties at this job will be to purchase all of our office supplies. There is a huge store called Office World over on Lemon St. Please go there sometime today.

We need 1 box of red pens, 1 box of pencils, 2 cases of printer paper, and 5 metal clipboards. Also buy an electric pencil sharpener. Tom's broke yesterday.

Just pay for it yourself, and we will pay you back. PLEASE GET A COPY OF THE RECEIPT. Give the receipt to Trina Lin. She'll make sure you are paid by tomorrow. She will add on $5.00 for gas money.

Thank you,
Terence

Source 2

Office World
1303 Lemon St.

RECEIPT OF PURCHASE

6/8/16   3:03 p.m.

AMOUNT	ITEM	PRICE
1	elec pencil sharpener	$15.00
2	printer paper (case)	$40.00
1	pens (box, red)	$5.00
5	clipboard (metal)	$10.00
	TOTAL COST	$70.00

Source 3

Driving Directions

From:
384 Apple Lane

To:
1303 Lemon Street

Distance:
3.2 miles

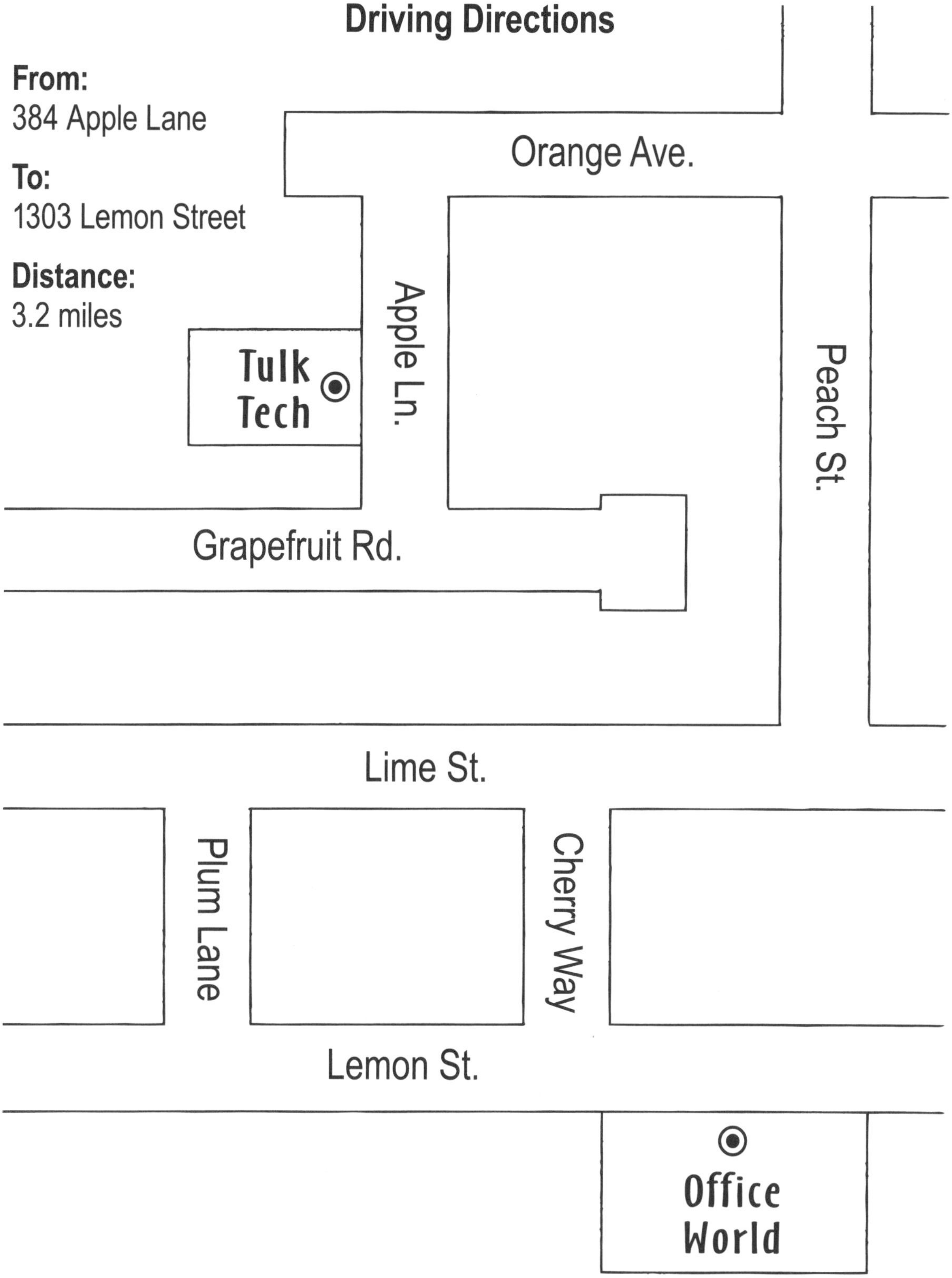

Orange Ave.

Apple Ln.

Peach St.

Tulk Tech ⊙

Grapefruit Rd.

Lime St.

Plum Lane

Cherry Way

Lemon St.

⊙ Office World

Supply the Answer *(cont.)*

Name: _____

Part 1: Read each idea. Which source gives you this information? Fill in the correct bubble for each source. (Note: More than one bubble may be filled in for each idea.)

Information	Sources ➡	1	2	3
1. Office World is located on Lemon Street.		○	○	○
2. Office World's address is 1303 Lemon Street.		○	○	○
3. Office World sells printer paper.		○	○	○

Part 2: Fill in the bubble next to the best answer to each question.

4. In what form is the information in Source 1 given?

    Ⓐ a handwritten letter

    Ⓑ an e-mail

    Ⓒ a purchase receipt

    Ⓓ a map of the neighborhood

5. Of these people, whose last name are we given?

    Ⓐ Trevor   Ⓒ Trina

    Ⓑ Terence   Ⓓ Tom

6. What is the most likely reason why "PLEASE GET A COPY OF THE RECEIPT" is written in all capital letters?

    Ⓐ Trevor feels that this is very important information.

    Ⓑ Terence feels that this is very important information.

    Ⓒ Tom needs to pay for his broken pencil sharpener.

    Ⓓ It is Trevor's first week at Tulk Tech.

Part 3: Search <u>Source 2</u> of "Supply the Answer" to find one example of the following:

7. the name of a strong material things are made of _____

Supply the Answer *(cont.)*

Name: _____

Part 4: Use the sources to answer the following questions.

8. Use Source 3 to give Trevor directions to Office World. Write each driving direction below. For each driving direction, give the name of the street and the direction Trevor will need to turn. The first two have been done for you.

❶ <u>Turn left onto Apple Lane.</u> _____

❷ <u>Turn right onto Orange Ave.</u> _____

❸ _____

❹ _____

❺ _____

❻ _____

9. Based on Sources 1 and 2, how much money will Trina make sure Trevor is paid by the next day?

_____

Explain how you came up with this answer. _____

_____

_____

_____

_____

_____

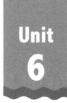

Supply the Answer (cont.)

Name: _____

Part 4 (cont.):

10. Trevor forgot to buy one supply. Use the sources to figure out which supply he forgot to buy. Then write a short e-mail from Terence to Trevor. In a nice way, tell Trevor what he forgot to buy.

From	terence@tulktech.com
To	trevor@tulktech.com
Date	June 9, 2016
Subject	office supplies

Trevor,

_____

_____

_____

_____

_____

_____

_____

_____

Thank you,

Terence

An Insect Emerges

Read each source below and on page 32. Then complete the activities on pages 33–35.

Source 1

Insects are everywhere! These small animals make up over half of all the living things on Earth. But not all creepy crawlies are insects. Worms are not insects. Neither are spiders or snails. To be an insect, an adult animal must have three body parts and six legs.

The front part of an adult insect is its **head**. An insect's head has two **antennae** on it. Antennae are often long and thin. Some insects use them to touch, taste, or smell.

The middle part is the **thorax**. Every insect has six legs. All six legs are connected to its thorax.

The back part is the **abdomen**. This part is often much bigger than the head and the thorax.

Source 2

Ella Reed was very excited. She told her mom, "I got butterfly!"

Her mom smiled. "What happened? Tell me more."

Ella paused to catch her breath. "We are doing insect reports in Mrs. Hill's class. I really wanted to do mine on butterflies, but Mrs. Hill picked names out of a hat. When she was picking for the butterfly report, I wished she'd pick my name. And she did! I couldn't believe it!"

"Wow, that's great! Your name emerged from the hat at just the right time," said her mother. "What insect did your brother get?"

"I think he got ants. He wanted spiders, but Mrs. Hill told him that spiders are not insects. I wonder why not. They look like insects."

Source 3

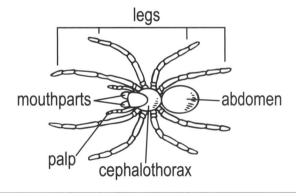

Parts of a Spider

legs

mouthparts

abdomen

palp

cephalothorax

Source 4

The Life Cycle of a Butterfly

by Ella Reed

Have you ever watched a butterfly? They are beautiful and colorful. They fly gracefully.

If you have watched a butterfly, then you have looked at an adult insect. All butterflies are adults. Butterflies go through four stages in life. These stages are called their life cycle.

Stage 1 – Egg
A butterfly's life begins inside an egg. Its mother often leaves the egg on a leaf. That way, when the baby hatches, it will have food nearby.

Stage 2 – Larva
This word is pronounced "**lar-vuh.**" In this stage, these insects don't have wings. They can't fly. They look more like worms than butterflies. They are caterpillars. During this stage, the insect eats a lot and grows a lot.

Stage 3 – Pupa
This word is pronounced "**pyoo-puh.**" At this stage, the insect forms a covering around itself. This covering is sometimes called a cocoon. A lot happens inside that cocoon. An adult butterfly begins to form.

Stage 4 – Adult
When the cocoon breaks open, an adult butterfly **emerges**. It comes out. It has large, beautiful wings. It has three main body parts and six legs. It has two antennae. When an adult lays an egg, the life cycle is complete.

An Insect Emerges *(cont.)*

Name: _____

Part 1: Read each idea. Which source gives you this information? Fill in the correct bubble for each source. (Note: More than one bubble may be filled in for each idea.)

Information	Sources ➡	1	2	3	4
1. Insects have antennae.		○	○	○	○
2. Spiders have palps.		○	○	○	○
3. Butterflies are adult insects.		○	○	○	○

Part 2: Fill in the bubble next to the best answer to each question.

4. When Ella's brother was first told that his report would be on ants, how did he probably feel?

Ⓐ disappointed   Ⓒ angry

Ⓑ disgusted   Ⓓ excited

5. In Source 2, it says, "Ella paused to catch her breath." What does this mean?

Ⓐ She used a butterfly net to trap an insect.

Ⓑ She tried to calm herself down so she could speak.

Ⓒ She quickly began her story about school.

Ⓓ She waited for her mother to ask more questions.

6. From Sources 2 and 4, you can tell that the word *emerges* means

Ⓐ "comes out."   Ⓒ "forms a cocoon."

Ⓑ "grows a lot."   Ⓓ "flies gracefully."

Part 3: Search Source 2 of "An Insect Emerges" to find one example of the following:

7. a piece of clothing _____

An Insect Emerges *(cont.)*

Name: _____

Part 4: Use the sources to answer the following questions.

8. Finish the pictures.

    A. This insect is missing legs, antennae, and an abdomen. Add these things to the drawing.

    B. The picture below shows the life cycle of a butterfly. It is missing two drawings and one label. Add the drawings and the missing word.

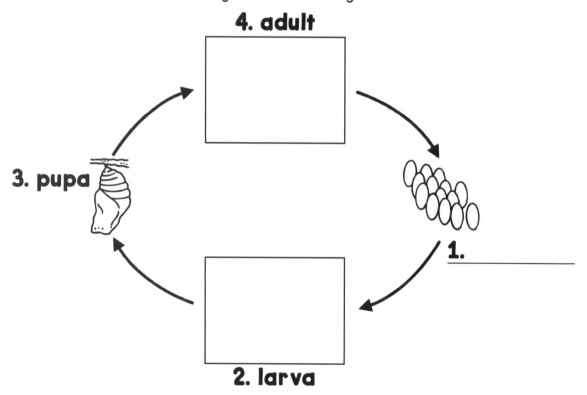

4. adult

3. pupa

1. _____

2. larva

An Insect Emerges *(cont.)*

Name: _____

Part 4 *(cont.):*

9. In Source 2, Ella wonders why spiders are not insects. Use what you have learned about insects and spiders to explain the answer to her.

_____

_____

_____

_____

10. Finish the story below.

If I were in Mrs. Hill's class, the insect I would want to

do a report on is _____.

This insect is interesting because _____

_____

_____

> *Here is a picture of my insect.*

_____.

The insect I would **not** want to do a report on is _____.

The reason for this is _____

_____

_____

_____.

Stop and Go

Read each source of information. Then complete the activities on pages 37–39.

Source 1

synonym
noun

a word that means the same thing (or nearly the same thing) as another word

Pronounced: **sin-ō-nim**

Examples:

- **stop** — finish, end, halt, cease, conclude

- **go** — begin, move, leave, disappear, depart

Source 2

I had just finished eating breakfast. I was reading and enjoying a quiet day. Then something happened. A loud noise broke the silence. I looked out the window.

I observed a jam on the street below. A big truck had halted the traffic. It had blocked other cars from going. The drivers of the other cars were honking their horns. The honking was so loud! It felt like the horrible noise would never cease. Finally, the truck got out of the way. The other cars began moving. The quiet returned.

Source 3

We <u>go</u> on our bicycles. We come to a road. A sign stops us. It reads, "Do Not <u>Go In</u>."

I <u>go</u> to say, "Tammy, we have to <u>go</u>."

Tammy stops me and says, "Timmy, we can make this sign <u>go away</u>. We can hide it in the bushes over there."

I turn my bike around. "That is not a good idea," I say. "We should <u>go</u>."

Tammy nods, and we <u>go</u>.

Stop and Go *(cont.)*

Name: _____

Part 1: The word "stop" or "stopped" never appears in Source 2, but five synonyms for these words are used. Fill out the chart with those synonyms. Tell what was "stopped" when that synonym appeared in the story. The first two are done for you.

	Synonym for "Stop" or "Stopped"	**What Was Stopped**
Example:	finished	eating
Example:	broke	silence
1.		
2.		
3.		

Part 2: Fill in the bubble next to the best answer to each question.

4. An antonym is a word that means the opposite of another word. Which word from Source 2 is an antonym of *stopped*?

Ⓐ happened   Ⓒ began

Ⓑ blocked   Ⓓ got

5. When Tammy nods at the end of Source 3, she is _____ Timmy.

Ⓐ agreeing with   Ⓒ going away from

Ⓑ disagreeing with   Ⓓ stopping

Part 3: Search <u>Source 3</u> of "Stop and Go" to find one example of each of the following:

6. a word that **begins** with two vowels _____

7. a word that **ends** with two vowels _____

Stop and Go *(cont.)*

Name: _____

Part 4: Use the sources to answer the following questions.

8. Most stories have a beginning, a middle, and an end. What happens in each part of Source 2?

Beginning: _____

_____

_____

Middle: _____

_____

_____

End: _____

_____

_____

9. Source 2 uses many synonyms, while Source 3 repeats one word ("go") many times. In your opinion, which way of writing makes the story more enjoyable for the reader? Explain your answer.

_____

_____

_____

_____

_____

_____

Name: _____

Part 4 *(cont.):*

10. Try rewriting Source 3. This time, use synonyms in place of the underlined words and phrases. Use a different synonym each time.

We _____ on our bicycles.

We come to a road. A sign stops us. It reads,

"Do Not _____."

I _____ to say, "Tammy,

we have to _____."

Tammy stops me and says, "Timmy, we can make this sign

_____. We can hide it

in the bushes over there."

I turn my bike around. "That is not a good idea," I say.

"We should _____."

Tammy nods, and we _____.

Sign Language

Read each source below and on page 41. Then complete the activities on pages 42–43.

Source 1

> ## narrator
>
> the person recounting (telling) the events of a story
>
> Sometimes, a narrator is a character in a story.

Source 2

Common Road Signs *(Each sign's meaning is written above it.)*

Stop

Yield

School Zone

You can only drive
in one direction.

The road ahead
is curvy.

A train might
pass through.

Animals may
cross the road.

My little sister asks a lot of questions. She wants to know everything. When we're driving someplace new, she distracts Mom. Mom says, "Sorry, Tess, I need to focus on the road. Tony, tell your sister the answer."

It is a big job. My sister has to ask about every road sign we pass.

"What's that red triangle sign say?" she asks.

"It says 'Yield.' That means Mom has to make sure nobody else is going. Then she can go."

"Why does the yellow diamond sign have a pretty deer on it?"

"See how there are woods on both sides of the road? I guess deer live in these woods. Mom has to watch out for deer. They may try to cross the road in front of her."

"That triangle square sign has a mama and a child."

"That shape is called a pentagon. It has five sides. That sign means that there is a school nearby. Children might be crossing the street."

Tess pointed, "What's that sign? It's a circle with a big X on it. It has two R letters on it."

I had never seen that sign before. Mom quickly answered. "That is a railroad crossing sign. That means a train could come through on those tracks ahead."

"I want to see a train!" my sister yelled. I think it took Mom and me an hour to calm Tess down. She kept asking, "When are we going to see a train?"

Sign Language *(cont.)*

Name: _____

Part 1: Read each idea. Which source gives you this information? Fill in the correct bubble for each source. (Note: More than one bubble may be filled in for each idea.)

Information	Sources ➡	1	2	3
1. The yield sign is triangle-shaped.		○	○	○
2. The yield sign is red.		○	○	○
3. A pentagon has five sides.		○	○	○

Part 2: Fill in the bubble next to the best answer to each question.

4. Who is the narrator of Source 3?

    Ⓐ Mom   Ⓒ Tony

    Ⓑ the little brother   Ⓓ Tess

5. Which sign would you most likely see at the beginning of a twisting mountain road?

  Ⓐ    Ⓑ 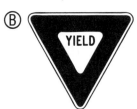   Ⓒ    Ⓓ

6. Which statement about Source 3 is true?

    Ⓐ Tess knows all of her shapes.

    Ⓑ Tess knows some of her shapes.

    Ⓒ Tess cannot read any letters or words.

    Ⓓ Mom never answers Tess's questions.

Part 3: Search <u>Source 3</u> of "Sign Language" to find the name of the following:

7. a shape that has no straight sides _____

Name: _____

Part 4: Use the sources to answer the following questions.

8. Look at the five road signs below. Follow these instructions:

   ▶ Cross out the one that was not mentioned in Source 3.

   ▶ Put the remaining signs in order from 1–4 by when they appeared in Source 3. Write "1" on the line below the sign that was mentioned first.

_____   _____   _____   _____   _____

9. Choose one of the signs from Source 2 that is **not** mentioned in Source 3. Imagine that Tess is asking you what that sign means. Write the question Tess might ask about the sign. Then tell her what the sign means.

Tess: _____

_____

You: _____

_____

10. How would Source 3 be different if Tess were the narrator? Explain your answer. What kind of thoughts might Tess have about her mother and her brother?

_____

_____

_____

_____

The Fast and the Slow

Read each source below and on page 45. Then complete the activities on pages 46–47.

Source 1

Did you know that cheetahs are the fastest animals on land? Their bodies are made for sprinting. Their bodies are light and lean. This helps cheetahs gain speed quickly.

A cheetah has a very flexible spine. This allows the cheetah to bend its back a lot as it runs. A cheetah has a long, flat tail. This allows a cheetah to turn suddenly at high speeds.

A cheetah's claws are always out. Its claws are never covered by skin or fur. Most other cats don't have this type of claw. These special claws are great for gripping the ground as the cheetah runs.

These features make cheetahs great hunters. They help cheetahs chase down prey on the grasslands where they live.

Source 2

grasslands — a large, open area of country covered with grass and low shrubs

Animals such as cheetahs, antelopes, and zebras live in grassland areas.

Source 3

World's Fastest Animals on Land

Animal	Miles Per Hour (mph)
Cheetah	70
Antelope	60
Lion	50

World's Slowest Animals on Land

Animal	Miles Per Hour (mph)
Snail	0.03 mph
Sloth	0.15 mph
Tortoise	0.17 mph

Source 4

Sloths live in trees. They spend most of their time hanging upside-down. They don't move much. When they do move, they do so very slowly. Sloths are made for this kind of living.

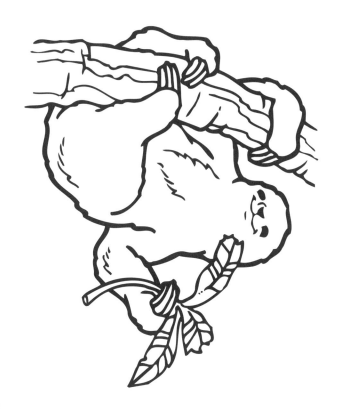

1. Sloths mostly eat leaves.

2. They have long, curved claws. These help sloths hang upside-down from tree branches.

3. Their fur is brown. Tiny green plants grow on it. These two colors make it difficult for other animals to see sloths on trees.

4. Their fur grows in the opposite direction than most other animals' fur. This keeps rainwater and other things from clinging to a sloth's fur as it hangs upside-down.

The Fast and the Slow (cont.)

Name: _____

Part 1: Read each idea. Which source gives you this information? Fill in the correct bubble for each source. (Note: More than one bubble may be filled in for each idea.)

Information Sources ➡	1	2	3	4
1. Cheetahs live in grassland areas.	○	○	○	○
2. Cheetahs are fast-moving animals.	○	○	○	○
3. Sloths are slow-moving animals.	○	○	○	○

Part 2: Fill in the bubble next to the best answer to each question.

4. Which statement about cheetahs is **not** true?

   Ⓐ They have special claws.

   Ⓑ They live in trees.

   Ⓒ They are faster than lions.

   Ⓓ They hunt other animals.

5. Which of these words from Source 1 means "running really fast"?

   Ⓐ sprinting   Ⓒ gripping

   Ⓑ flexible   Ⓓ suddenly

6. Source 1 tells us that cheetahs have flexible spines. Which of these things could also be called flexible?

   Ⓐ a piece of brick

   Ⓑ a piece of glass

   Ⓒ a piece of hard plastic

   Ⓓ a piece of soft rubber

Part 3: Search <u>Source 4</u> of "The Fast and the Slow" to find the following:

7. a word that means "holding on to tightly" _____

The Fast and the Slow *(cont.)*

Name: _____

Part 4: Use the sources to answer the following questions.

8. The title of this unit is "The Fast and the Slow." If it had been called "The Fastest and the Slowest," then Source 4 would probably have been about which animal? Circle your answer. Then explain your answer on the lines below.

antelope   **snail**   **tortoise**   **lion**

_____

_____

9. Compare and contrast the cheetah and the sloth. Name one way that cheetahs and sloths are different. Then name one way in which they are the same.

_____

_____

_____

10. Source 1 and Source 4 both give information about animals. They do this in different ways. Source 1 is a passage of writing. Source 4 uses a numbered list. Which way made it easier for you to learn the information? Why do you think that is?

_____

_____

_____

An Ancient Puzzle

Read each source of information. Then complete the activities on pages 49–51.

Source 1

Eddie was playing with wooden puzzle pieces. He was using the pieces to form a picture. He formed a picture of a rabbit.

Kim asked, "What game is that? What are you playing?"

Eddie said, "This is called a tangram. It is an old game. Tangrams have been around for a long time."

"Can you use the pieces to make something other than a rabbit?"

Eddie nodded, "Yes. You can make thousands of things!"

"With just those few pieces?" Kim asked, "Can you make a cat?"

Source 2

ancient

having been around for a very long time; very old

Source 3

The Seven Pieces of the Tangram

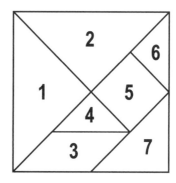

Each piece is called a **tan**.

Source 4

A tangram is a puzzle. It is made up of seven pieces. The pieces fit together to make one large square. They can also be used to form many other shapes. In fact, over 6,500 shapes can be made from just these seven pieces.

Some are in the shapes of animals.

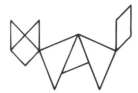

Some are in the shapes of people.

Some are in the shapes of objects.

Tangrams were first used in China hundreds of years ago. The Chinese word for *tangram* means "seven boards of skill."

An Ancient Puzzle *(cont.)*

Name: _____

Part 1: Read each idea. Which source gives you this information? Fill in the correct bubble for each source. (Note: More than one bubble may be filled in for each idea.)

Information	Sources ➡	1	2	3	4
1. Tangrams have been around a long time.		○	○	○	○
2. Tangrams are made up of seven pieces.		○	○	○	○
3. Each piece of a tangram is called a *tan*.		○	○	○	○

Part 2: Fill in the bubble next to the best answer to each question.

4. Of the seven tans, how many are triangles?

ⓐ 3   ⓒ 5

ⓑ 4   ⓓ 6

5. Of the numbered triangles in Source 3, which two are the same size and shape?

ⓐ 1 and 7   ⓒ 2 and 4

ⓑ 6 and 7   ⓓ 4 and 6

6. Find shape #3 in Source 3. That shape is used to make which part of the cat picture in Source 4?

ⓐ tail   ⓒ head

ⓑ body   ⓓ ear

Part 3: Search <u>Source 4</u> of "An Ancient Puzzle" to find one example of the following:

7. the name of a country _____

An Ancient Puzzle *(cont.)*

Name: _____

Part 4: Look at each shape. Tell what it is. Tell if it is a **person**, **animal**, or **object**. Then write in the shape numbers from Source 3. Some numbers have been written for you.

8. A.

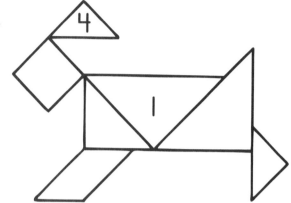

What is it? _____

Is it a person,

    animal, or object? _____

B.

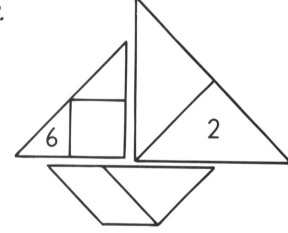

What is it? _____

Is it a person,

    animal, or object? _____

C.

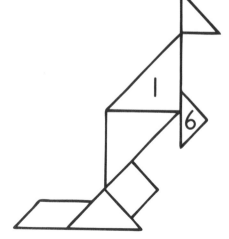

What is it? _____

Is it a person,

    animal, or object? _____

An Ancient Puzzle *(cont.)*

Name: _____

Part 5: Use the sources to answer these questions.

9. Make Source 1 longer. Add a few more lines. Have Eddie answer Kim's question. Have Kim ask another question about tangrams. Have Eddie answer that question, too.

Kim asked, "Can you make a cat?"

Eddie answered, " _____ ."

Then Kim asked, " _____ ?"

Eddie said, " _____ ."

10. Think of an animal or object that you would like to use a tangram to make. Choose one that isn't shown in this unit.

Write the name of the animal or object here: _____

> Now try to make it. Use only the "seven boards of skill."

Getting Enough Sleep

Read each source of information. Then complete the activities on pages 53–55.

Source 1

How much sleep does a person need each day? It depends on the age of the person. This graph shows how many hours a person needs to sleep.

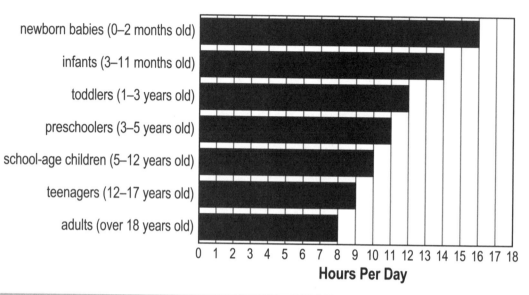

Hours Per Day

(Bar graph showing hours per day for each group)
- newborn babies (0–2 months old)
- infants (3–11 months old)
- toddlers (1–3 years old)
- preschoolers (3–5 years old)
- school-age children (5–12 years old)
- teenagers (12–17 years old)
- adults (over 18 years old)

Axis: 0 1 2 3 4 5 6 7 8 9 10 11 12 13 14 15 16 17 18

Source 2

I'm yawning. So is Dad. Mom is, too.

We are all yawning because of my new baby sister. Baby Grace is small in size, but she keeps big people from getting enough sleep. I'm seven years old. I am a big girl.

Grace cries half the night. I can't sleep. She sleeps all day. I can't play. Mom says I'm too loud. Mom says, "Be quieter, Jen. The baby is sleeping!"

Dad said he slept four hours last night. Mom slept less than that. I think I slept about seven hours. Is that enough?

The only one of us getting a lot of sleep is Grace. Mom writes down how much Grace sleeps each day. I need sleep, too! Who is writing down how much sleep I am getting?

Source 3

Baby Grace's Sleep Schedule

Times Asleep	Hours Slept
12:00 a.m. to 3:00 a.m.	3
4:00 a.m. to 7:00 a.m.	3
7:30 a.m. to 9:30 a.m.	2
12:00 p.m. to 4:00 p.m.	4
7:30 p.m. to 11:30 p.m.	4

Part 1: According to Source 1, which of these people needs more sleep? Write the correct symbol on each line. Write **>** (greater than), **<** (less than), or **=** (equal to).

1. a 7-year-old _____ a 14-year-old

2. a 6-month-old _____ an infant

3. a 6-year-old _____ an infant

Part 2: Fill in the bubble next to the best answer to each question.

4. According to Source 1, how many more hours does a newborn baby need to sleep than an infant needs to sleep?

Ⓐ 1   Ⓒ 3

Ⓑ 2   Ⓓ 4

5. The third sentence of Source 2 is "Mom is, too." What is Mom doing in that sentence?

Ⓐ yawning

Ⓑ sleeping

Ⓒ crying

Ⓓ telling Jen to be quiet

6. Who is telling the story in Source 2?

Ⓐ Grace

Ⓑ Grace's sister

Ⓒ Grace's mother

Ⓓ Grace's father

Part 3: Search <u>Source 2</u> of "Getting Enough Sleep" to find the following:

7. a word that means "less noisy" _____

Name: _____

Part 4: Use the sources to answer the following questions.

8. Based on Source 3, how many total hours did Grace sleep? _____

Is that enough sleep for a person her age? Use the information you have been given to explain your answer.

_____

_____

_____

_____

9. Look at the two boldfaced statements. Based on the information given, which one is true?

**We need more sleep
as we get older.**

**We need more sleep
when we are younger.**

Now tell why you think this might be true. (**Hint:** There are no wrong answers!)

_____

_____

_____

_____

_____

Getting Enough Sleep *(cont.)*

Name: _____

Part 4 *(cont.)*:

10. Write a short story that is like Source 2. This time, choose a different family member to tell the story. Write the story as if you are Mom, Dad, or Baby Grace.

Name of the person telling the story: _____

_____

_____

_____

_____

_____

_____

_____

_____

_____

_____

_____

_____

_____

The Baker's Dozen

Read each source of information. Then complete the activities on pages 57–59.

Source 1

It was a Saturday morning. Mom sent me to The Baker's Dozen Donut Shop. She had never let me go by myself before! She said, "Lily, here is $10 for a dozen donuts. You can even choose the flavors!"

I left my house at 8:15. The donut shop is very close to our house. It took me exactly five minutes to walk there.

When it was my turn to order, I asked for a dozen donuts. First, I ordered three cinnamon rolls. My dad loves those. Then, I ordered four donuts with chocolate sprinkles. Lastly, I ordered five donuts with pink frosting. The man behind the counter put all of these donuts into a large box.

I thought I was done. I had ordered 12 donuts. The man said, "You can choose one more donut." I thought to myself, "Should I tell him that 3 + 4 + 5 = 12?" Instead, I chose a long bar with fudge stripes on it. It looked yummy.

As I walked home, I thought about eating one of the donuts. Mom wouldn't miss one pink-frosted donut, would she? After all, she only told me to get a dozen donuts.

Source 2

dozen — twelve of something

baker's dozen — thirteen of something

Source 3

I can't believe how grown up Lily is now. I remember the first time her mother came to my donut shop. She was pushing Lily in a baby stroller. For years, her mother stopped by every Tuesday morning to buy a box of donuts. As Lily got older, her mother would always choose at least one donut with pink frosting for Lily.

Today, Lily came in all by herself to order a dozen donuts. She looked very surprised when I gave her a 13th donut. We are called The Baker's Dozen for a reason. We have always given customers a free donut when they buy a dozen.

I could tell by the look in Lily's eye that she thought I couldn't add very well. I wonder if she'll eat that 13th donut on her way home!

Name: _____

Part 1: Read each idea about The Baker's Dozen Donut Shop. Which source gives you this information? Fill in the correct bubble for each source.

Information	Sources ➡	1	2	3
1. The Baker's Dozen is near Lily's house.		○	○	○
2. Lily has been going to this donut shop her whole life.		○	○	○
3. A box of donuts costs no more than $10 there.		○	○	○

Part 2: Fill in the bubble next to the best answer to each question.

4. From the information given, what do we know about Lily's father?

   Ⓐ He works on Tuesdays.

   Ⓑ He doesn't eat donuts.

   Ⓒ He likes cinnamon rolls.

   Ⓓ He's never been to The Baker's Dozen.

5. Which clock shows the time that Lily **arrived** at the donut shop in Source 1?

Ⓐ    Ⓑ    Ⓒ    Ⓓ

6. What "look" does the shop owner see in Lily's eye in Source 3?

   Ⓐ She thinks he has mistakenly given her too many donuts.

   Ⓑ She thinks he has mistakenly given her too much money back.

   Ⓒ She thinks the pink donuts look larger than usual.

   Ⓓ She thinks he hasn't given her as many donuts as she should be getting.

Part 3: Search <u>Source 3</u> of "The Baker's Dozen" to find of the following:

7. a word that rhymes with "clocks" _____

The Baker's Dozen *(cont.)*

Name: _____

Part 4: Use the sources to answer the following questions.

8. On which day of the week does Source 3 take place? Circle the correct answer. Then explain how you know this answer.

Tuesday   **Saturday**   **Sunday**

_____

_____

_____

_____

9. Do you think Lily's mother will notice if Lily eats the 13th donut before she gets home? Why or why not? Use complete sentences in your answer.

_____

_____

_____

_____

_____

_____

_____

Name: _____

Part 4 *(cont.)*:

10. In the box below, draw the donuts Lily bought in Source 1. Use the information in Source 1 to decorate them correctly. The three cinnamon rolls have already been put in the box.

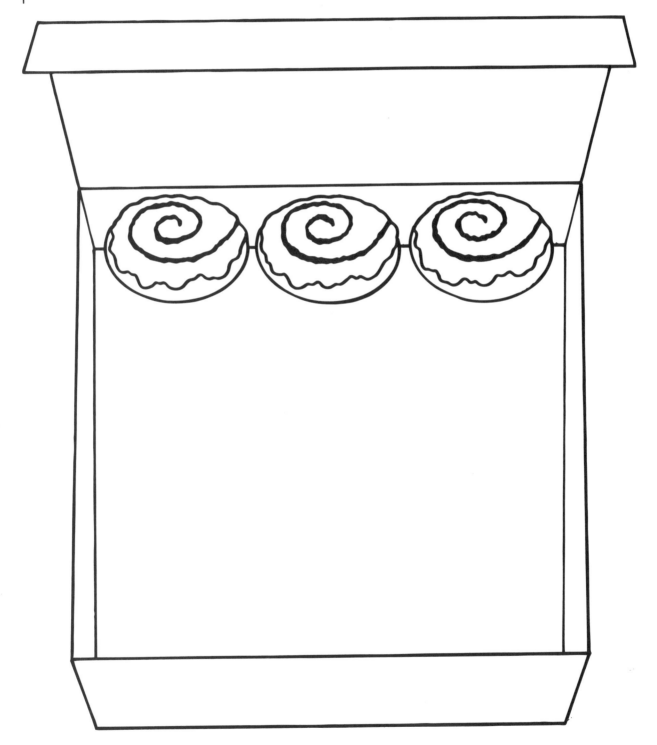

Extra Extra!

Read each source of information. Then complete the activities on pages 61–63.

Source 1

New at Pete's Pizza Palace

THE EXTRANORMOUS

An enormous pizza at an extra enormous value! Each slice is a meal!

Just $20

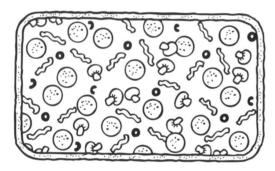

* *Price is for cheese pizza only.*
Add $2 for each extra topping.

Source 2

Guest List for Lisa's Party

Ashley — cheese

Brittany — cheese

Carla — cheese

Kevin — cheese

Kelly — pepperoni

Lisa — pepperoni

Jack — pepperoni

Maria — pepperoni

Nicky — pepperoni

Philip — mushrooms

Zoe — mushrooms

Source 3

Ordering a pizza can be complicated! I asked Lisa to give me a list of everyone who is coming to her birthday party. I also asked her to tell me what kind of pizza each person likes. She wrote this information next to each person's name.

It looks like some people just want cheese. Some want pepperoni. Others want mushrooms. I will order the Extranormous pizza from Pete's Pizza Palace. I will get it with two extra toppings.

I have a lot of people to feed, but this pizza is supposed to be extra enormous. I hope it will do the trick! There might even be a piece left over for me. The birthday girl's mom should get to eat too, right? I'll take a slice of mushroom pizza if I can.

Name: _____

Part 1: Read each idea. Which source gives you this information? Fill in the correct bubble for each source. (Note: More than one bubble may be filled in for each idea.)

Information	Sources ➡	1	2	3
1. Pete's Pizza Palace sells an "Extranormous" pizza.		○	○	○
2. Lisa likes pepperoni on her pizza.		○	○	○
3. Lisa's mom likes mushrooms on her pizza.		○	○	○

Part 2: Fill in the bubble next to the best answer to each question.

   4. Complete this sentence: If you get extra of something, you get _____ of it.

    Ⓐ more   Ⓒ enormous

    Ⓑ less   Ⓓ each

   5. In what order are the names written in Source 2?

    Ⓐ in alphabetical order

    Ⓑ in order by type of pizza

    Ⓒ in girl/boy order

    Ⓓ by how good of a friend each person is to Lisa

   6. What is the main purpose of the 2nd paragraph in Source 3?

    Ⓐ to name the people who will be invited to Lisa's party

    Ⓑ to talk about how good the pizza is at Pete's Pizza Palace

    Ⓒ to tell what toppings the pizza needs to have on it

    Ⓓ to tell how much the pizza for the party will cost

Part 3: Search <u>Source 3</u> of "Extra Extra" to find one example of the following:

   7. a word that has four syllables and means "confusing and difficult" _____

Extra Extra! *(cont.)*

Name: _____

Part 4: Use the sources to answer the following questions.

8. **A.** Use tally marks to complete this chart. Show the number of slices needed with each topping. Only use the information given in Source 2. The first column is done for you.

Cheese	Mushrooms	Pepperoni
||||		

B. If each pizza has 12 slices, will there be a piece left over for Lisa's mom?

_____

C. Draw the topping needed on each slice of the pizza below.

▶ Draw pepperoni circles on the slices that need them.

▶ Draw mushroom pieces on the slices that need them.

▶ Leave the cheese slices blank.

Don't forget to make a slice for Lisa's mom!

Extra Extra! *(cont.)*

Name: _____

Part 4 *(cont.)***:** Use the sources to answer these questions.

9. Look back at the pizza you made on the previous page. How much will that "Extranormous" pizza cost?

Write the total here: _____

Now explain where you found the information you needed to answer this question?

_____

_____

_____

_____

10. Use only Source 1 to answer these questions.

    A. Which one word in this source is not a real word?

    Write it here: _____

    B. What two words are combined to make this word?

    Write them here: _____ _____

    C. Can you think of two other words that could be combined to make a word that means the same thing?

    Write them here: _____ _____

    D. What would this new word be?

    Write it here: _____

Show Their Stripes

Read each source of information. Then complete the activities on pages 65–67.

Source 1

The A to Z of Zebras
by Amber Zisk

Most of us think of stripes when we think of zebras. Zebras have a beautiful pattern of black and white stripes on their faces and bodies. These stripes help them hide in the tall grass where they live. This helps them to survive and stay away from **predators**. Predators are animals that hunt other animals. The cheetah is one animal that hunts zebras.

Did you know that no two zebras have the same stripe pattern? Each zebra's stripe pattern is unique.

Zebras live mostly on the continent of Africa. They like to live in large groups, and they sleep standing up. Zebras eat grasses and leaves. They do not eat meat.

Source 2

Ari tapped on the glass of his aquarium. "Take a look at that beauty," he said.

Zoe asked, "Is that your new fish? I like his blue stripes. What kind is he?"

"That," said Ari, "is a zebrafish."

"Because of his stripes!" smiled Zoe.

"You're right!" laughed Ari. "But did you know that every zebrafish has exactly five blue stripes. The stripes are **horizontal**. They go across the length of the fish's body. They go from its head to its tail."

"I did not know that," said Zoe.

Source 3

"The zebras called a good game today," said Zoe. "My team lost fair and square."

"Zebras?" asked Ari. "Didn't you just watch a football game? I don't understand sports. What were zebras doing on the field?"

Zoe laughed. "That's what people call the referees. Referees are the people who make sure the players follow the rules."

"Why do people call them 'zebras'?"

"You would know if you saw them," said Zoe. "They wear special uniforms so that everyone can see them. If the referees looked like the players, that would be confusing. Every referee wears a shirt that has big black and white stripes on it. The stripes are always **vertical**. The stripes go up and down."

Show Their Stripes (cont.)

Name: _____

Part 1: Read each idea. Which source gives you this information? Fill in the correct bubble for each source.

Information	Sources ➡	1	2	3
1. Ari owns an aquarium.		○	○	○
2. Amber wrote a report on zebras.		○	○	○
3. Zoe has a favorite football team.		○	○	○

Part 2: Fill in the bubble next to the best answer to each question.

4. Which part of Source 1 tells us that a zebra's stripe pattern is one-of-a-kind?

   Ⓐ the title

   Ⓑ the first paragraph

   Ⓒ the second paragraph

   Ⓓ the caption under the picture

5. What does it mean if a game is played "fair and square"?

   Ⓐ Nobody won.   Ⓒ Nobody cheated.

   Ⓑ Nobody lost.   Ⓓ Nobody was confused.

6. Which fact from Source 1 tells us that zebras are **not** predators?

   Ⓐ They do not eat meat.

   Ⓑ They live in large groups.

   Ⓒ They sleep standing up.

   Ⓓ They have unique stripe patterns.

Part 3: Search Source 1 of "Show Their Stripes" to find the following:

7. a word made from scrambling the letters in "team" _____

Name: _____

Part 4: Use the sources to answer the following questions.

8. Name two ways that grasses help zebras to survive.

_____

_____

_____

_____

_____

9. Name one way that a zebra's stripes and a referee's stripes are the same. Name one way that they are different.

Same	Different

Show Their Stripes (cont.)

Name: _____

Part 4 (cont.):

10. Look at each picture below. Make the blank shirt a referee's uniform. Make the blank fish a zebrafish.

Then circle **horizontal** or **vertical** to show which kind of stripes you added to each picture.

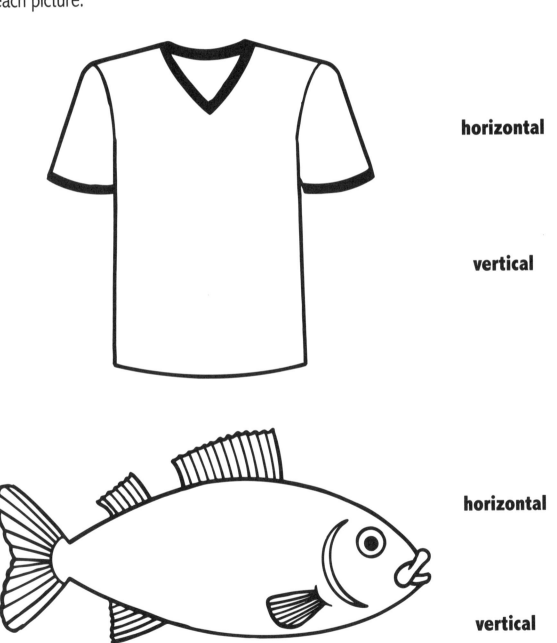

horizontal

vertical

horizontal

vertical

Sharing a Name

Read each source below and on page 69. Then complete the activities on pages 70–71.

Source 1

My name is Kira. I used to think I was the only one with that name. I have lived in Ohio my whole life. I was born in 2006. Nobody else around here had my name. Then I met another Kira. She moved here from New York in 2013. Kira and I became best friends.

Everyone calls us the "Kira Twins" even though we don't look alike. I have black hair, while my friend Kira has blond hair. I am even one year older than she is.

We are not alike in most ways. My favorite foods are hamburgers and hot dogs. Kira is a vegetarian. She mostly eats fruits and vegetables. She brings odd foods to lunch. Yesterday, she ate some strange fruit. I had never seen it before. It was brown and fuzzy on the outside. It was green with little black seeds on the inside. Kira ate the green part *and* the seeds! I didn't know you could do that. Kira said the fruit was called a kiwi.

Source 2

Fast Facts About Kiwifruits

☞ They were once called Chinese gooseberries.

☞ They came to the United States in 1959 from New Zealand. The name was changed at that time. The name "kiwi" was chosen because it was the name of New Zealand's national bird.

☞ Don't eat the fuzzy brown outside.

☞ The flesh on the inside is bright green and delicious.

☞ You can also eat the tiny black seeds inside the fruit.

☞ Kiwis are a great source of fiber and Vitamin C.

Source 3

Learning About New Zealand

New Zealand is a country. It is located near Australia in the Pacific Ocean. New Zealand is made up of several islands.

New Zealand is sometimes called "the land of the birds." Many of these birds cannot fly. One such flightless bird is the kiwi. The kiwi is the national bird of New Zealand.

Source 4

Fast Facts About Kiwi Birds

- They are covered in brown feathers.

- They cannot fly.

- They are the size of chickens.

- Their eggs are six times as big as chicken eggs.

- They have long beaks. A kiwi's nostrils are at the end of its beak. This is unlike all other birds. This helps kiwis have a stronger sense of smell than other birds.

- They use their long beaks to find worms that live under the ground. Kiwis eat worms, insects, seeds, and fruits.

- They come from New Zealand. The kiwi is the national bird of that country.

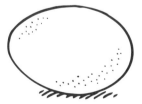

Name: _____

Part 1: Read each idea. Which source gives you this information? Fill in the correct bubble for each source. (Note: More than one bubble may be filled in for each idea.)

Information	Sources ➡	1	2	3	4
1. New Zealand is a country near Australia.		○	○	○	○
2. New Zealand's national bird is the kiwi.		○	○	○	○
3. Kiwi birds cannot fly.		○	○	○	○

Part 2: Fill in the bubble next to the best answer to each question.

4. Why do people call the two girls in Source 1 the "Kira Twins"?

Ⓐ because they look alike

Ⓑ because they like the same things

Ⓒ because they are friends who have the same name

Ⓓ because they are both from New York

5. Which statement is true?

Ⓐ The Kira Twins were named after each other.

Ⓑ The kiwifruit was named after the kiwi bird.

Ⓒ The kiwi bird was named after the kiwifruit.

Ⓓ New Zealand was named after New York.

6. Which word from the sources means "openings of the nasal cavity (or nose)"?

Ⓐ beaks   Ⓒ smell

Ⓑ flesh   Ⓓ nostrils

Part 3: Search <u>Source 2</u> of "Sharing a Name" to find one example of the following:

7. a country **not** named New Zealand _____

Sharing a Name *(cont.)*

Name: _____

Part 4: Use the sources to answer the following questions.

8. Name two ways that the "Kira Twins" are different from one another.

_____

_____

_____

9. Name two ways that the kiwi bird and the kiwifruit are alike.

_____

_____

_____

10. Look at these four things and people. Circle the one that was given its name first. Underline the one that was given its name last. On the lines below, explain how you answered this question.

Kira from Ohio   Kira from New York   kiwifruit   kiwi bird

_____

_____

_____

_____

_____

Write and Wrong

Read each source of information. Then complete the activities on pages 73–75.

Source 1

Homophones are words that sound the same but have different meanings.

Examples:

- **sea** and **see**

  I <u>see</u> three fish swimming in the <u>sea</u>.

- **right** and **write**

  Did Rita <u>write</u> the <u>right</u> name on the card?

- **to**, **too**, and **two**

  I plan <u>to</u> see that movie <u>two</u> times, <u>too</u>.

Source 2

Mr. Owl's Capitalization Rules

Capitalize the first letter of . . .

1. the first word in each sentence
2. the word "I"
3. a person's name
4. the name of a street, city, state, country, etc.
5. the name of a day, month, or holiday

Source 3

Dear Danny,

My trip is almost over. I can't wait to see you and Mom. I should fly back into the United states by halloween. What costume will you wear this year.

I talked to Mom about you yesterday. She sayed that you are becoming a very good reader and writer. I always new you would bee smart!

Please right back to me when you get a chance. i would love to hear from you. This trip has been fun, but I miss my little brother

Sea you soon,
Joey

P.S. I am sure you know this already, but I left a few mistakes in this letter. I did this on purpose to see how smart you are. Can you find all 10 errors?

Write and Wrong (cont.)

Name: _____

Part 1: Look at each of the five rules in Source 2. Which capitalization rules are being used in these sentences? Fill in the correct bubbles. (Note: More than one bubble will be filled in for each sentence.)

Sentence	Rule ➡	1	2	3	4	5
1. My family and I took a vacation.		O	O	O	O	O
2. In November, we drove to Canada.		O	O	O	O	O
3. We spent Thanksgiving with Ann's family.		O	O	O	O	O

Part 2: Fill in the bubble next to the best answer to each question.

4. Which two words from Joey's letter can have **opposite** meanings?

    Ⓐ *back* and *home*   Ⓒ *miss* and *fun*

    Ⓑ *left* and *right*   Ⓓ *soon* and *new*

5. Which two words from Joey's letter mean the **same** thing?

    Ⓐ *over* and *back*   Ⓒ *chance* and *purpose*

    Ⓑ *trip* and *fly*   Ⓓ *mistakes* and *errors*

6. What is the main purpose of the first paragraph of Joey's letter?

    Ⓐ to say that he will be coming home soon

    Ⓑ to say that he put mistakes in his letter

    Ⓒ to tell his brother that he misses him

    Ⓓ to tell his brother about homophones

Part 3: Search <u>Source 2</u> of "Write and Wrong" to find one example of the following:

7. a word with six syllables _____

Write and Wrong *(cont.)*

Name: _____

Part 4: Refer back to the sources, and use complete sentences to answer these questions.

8. Rewrite the first three paragraphs of Joey's letter from Source 3.

Do the following:

▶ Fix all 10 mistakes.

▶ Underline each word or punctuation mark that you corrected.

_____

_____

_____

_____

_____

_____

_____

_____

_____

_____

See you soon,
Joey

Part 4 *(cont.)*:

9. Look at the title of this unit. What do the words *write* and *wrong* have in common?

Hints:

▶ Think about how they are spelled.

▶ Think about how they are pronounced (how they sound when you say them).

_____

_____

_____

10. Write a short response from Danny to Joey. In your letter, use at least one set of homophones. Underline each homophone in your letter.

Dear Joey,

_____

_____

_____

_____

_____

_____

_____

Useful Machines

Read each source below and on page 77. Then complete the activities on pages 78–79.

Source 1

Simple Machines

Machines help us get work done. Many machines are **complex**. They are made of many parts. They need electricity to work. Cars and computers are two kinds of complex machines.

Some machines are **simple**, though. These machines do not need a lot of parts. They do not need electricity or engines. These kinds of machines have been around a long time. These were the first machines people used. People still use them today. Here are a few types of simple machines:

inclined plane

This allows you to move objects from one height up to another height. It creates a sloped surface. A ramp is an example.

lever

This uses a straight board to help you lift or move heavy objects. You put one end under the object while you push down on the other end.

screw

This has grooves built into it. When the screw is inserted into a material and turned, the grooves help move the material.

wedge

This is thicker at one end and narrower at the other. The narrow end can be used to split things or pry them apart. Tools such as axes and chisels are wedges.

wheel and axle

This allows you to move heavy things over long distances.

Source 2

	Sun.	Mon.	Tues.	Wed.	Thur.	Fri.	Sat.
March 1920		1	2	3	4	5	6
	7	8	9	10	11	12	13
	14	15	16	17	18	19	20
	21	22	23	24	25	26	27
	28	29	30	31			

Source 3

It was a Saturday morning. Chris ran up the basement stairs. He rushed into the kitchen. "Look what I found, Grandpa!" said Chris. "Is this photo really over 100 years old?"

Grandpa Mike took off his glasses. He took the photograph from Chris and held it very close to his face. He squinted. A smile broke out on Grandpa's face. "You bet it is! This picture was taken exactly 101 years ago."

Building a home. March 24, 1920.

"I was wondering where this picture had gone to," he said.

Chris sat and listened as his grandfather continued to speak. "That boy in the picture is my father. He was 10 years old at that time. These other men are his uncles. They are clearing the land to build a house. Uncle Jack is moving that big rock. He was a very strong man. Uncle Bill is chopping up that tree trunk. And that's Uncle Rex pushing that wheelbarrow and putting all that dirt into that container. They must have worked hard, but it was worth it. I grew up in the house that they were building that day."

Name: _____

Part 1: Use Source 2 to answer these questions. Write each answer on the line given.

1. How many Sundays were there in March in 1920?

_____

2. On which date was the first Friday of that month?

_____

3. On which day of the week was the picture in Source 3 taken?

_____

Part 2: Fill in the bubble next to the best answer to each question.

4. In what form is Source 2 given?

Ⓐ graph   Ⓒ story

Ⓑ calendar   Ⓓ description

5. Which of these would most likely have a sloped surface?

Ⓐ pizza   Ⓒ water slide

Ⓑ diving board   Ⓓ table top

6. The boy in the picture in Source 3 is Chris's

Ⓐ uncle.   Ⓒ grandfather.

Ⓑ father.   Ⓓ great-grandfather.

Part 3: Search <u>Source 3</u> of "Useful Machines" to find a word with the following meaning:

7. "to look through partly closed eyes" _____

Useful Machines *(cont.)*

Name: _____

Part 4: Use the sources to answer the following questions.

8. In what year does Source 3 take place? _____

How do you know this information?

_____

_____

9. There are three uncles doing work in the picture in Source 3. Complete the chart below. (Note: One uncle is using two types of machines.)

Type of Simple Machine	Name of Uncle	What It Is Helping Him Do

10. Choose one of the simple machines listed in Source 1. Give one example of how we still use this type of machine today.

_____

_____

_____

Time Will Tell

Read each source below and on page 81. Then complete the activities on pages 82–84.

Source 1

	a.m.	p.m.
Stands for	"ante meridiem"	"post meridiem"
Latin words that mean	"before mid-day"	"after mid-day"
Time of day	from midnight to 11:59 in morning	from noon to 11:59 at night

Source 2

I woke up in the middle of the night. It was **too** dark. I looked over at the purple panda clock next to my bed. It was dark, too. I got up and looked out of my window. The street outside our house was very dark. The streetlights were not working. None of the lights were on in our neighbors' houses.

Then suddenly, the lights outside turned on. I looked back at the clock next to my bed. The numbers on it were flashing. They looked like this:

I knew that time was not right. That is when I heard Mom's bedroom door open.

Source 3

Mom tucked me into bed. She said, "Sweet dreams, Lulu." The purple panda clock next to my bed showed the time.

My bedtime was supposed to be 9:00. Mom smiled and said, "It looks as though you're getting away with a late bedtime tonight. At least tomorrow is Saturday. We can sleep in a little later than usual."

Source 4

I walked down the hall and into the den. Mom was standing by the big clock. It looked like this:

Mom said, "That must have been the time when the electricity went out. I'm just glad my cell phone is still working. It shows that the time is 2:10."

Mom moved the hands on the big clock. Now they showed the correct time.

I asked, "What caused the power to go out?"

Mom yawned and said, "I don't know, but it's back on now. And it's time to go back to bed, Lulu. It's a good thing tomorrow is Saturday. We'll need the extra sleep now."

Name: _____

Part 1: Read each idea. Which source gives you this information? Fill in the correct bubble for each source. (Note: More than one bubble may be filled in for each idea.)

Information	Sources ➡	1	2	3	4
1. The child in the stories is named Lulu.		○	○	○	○
2. The child went to bed at 9:25.		○	○	○	○
3. The child has a purple panda clock.		○	○	○	○

Part 2: Fill in the bubble next to the best answer to each question.

4. Which of these shows the correct order in which the stories happened?

Ⓐ Source 2 ➡ Source 3 ➡ Source 4

Ⓑ Source 4 ➡ Source 3 ➡ Source 2

Ⓒ Source 3 ➡ Source 2 ➡ Source 4

Ⓓ Source 3 ➡ Source 4 ➡ Source 2

5. How long after Lulu's normal bedtime did her mother tuck her in?

Ⓐ 25 minutes   Ⓒ 15 minutes

Ⓑ 20 minutes   Ⓓ 5 minutes

6. Which is **not** true of the clock in Lulu's bedroom?

Ⓐ It is purple.

Ⓑ It has an hour hand and a minute hand.

Ⓒ It is shaped like a panda.

Ⓓ It is next to her bed.

Part 3: Search <u>Source 1</u> of "Time Will Tell" to find one example of the following:

7. a word that is spelled the same backwards and forwards _____

Time Will Tell *(cont.)*

Name: _____

Part 4: Use the sources to answer the following questions.

8. Answer these questions about Source 4.

   A. Who are the two main characters in these stories?

   _____   _____

   B. What was the main event that happened? Write a sentence.

   _____

   _____

   C. When did this event happen? Write a sentence. Use **a.m.** or **p.m.** in your answer.

   _____

   _____

   D. Why did this event happen? Write a sentence.

   _____

   _____

9. Did the electricity probably only go out in Lulu's house or in other houses in her neighborhood? Give a reason from the sources for your answer.

_____

_____

_____

_____

Name: _____

Part 4 *(cont.):*

10. Answer these questions about Sources 3 and 4.

A. On the clock below, show what time Lulu went to bed.

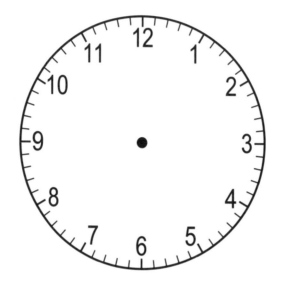

B. Is this time in the **a.m.** or **p.m.**? _____

C. On the clock below, show what time the electricity went out.

D. Is this time in the **a.m.** or **p.m.**? _____

E. How long after Lulu went to bed did the electricity go out?

_____

The Batting Order

Read each source below and on page 86. Then complete the activities on pages 87–89.

Source 1

There are nine positions on a starting baseball team. This diagram shows where they are located on the field.

Battery
C - catcher
P - pitcher

Infield
1B - first baseman
2B - second baseman
SS - shortstop
3B - third baseman

Outfield
LF - left fielder
CF - center fielder
RF - right fielder

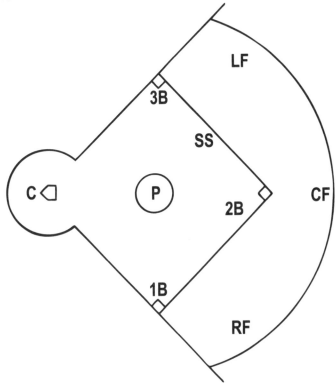

Other Terms

batting average – This number shows how often a player gets a hit. The best hitters usually have the highest batting averages.

batting order – This is the order in which the hitters on a team will bat.

home run – This is usually a ball hit high and far that goes over the outfield fence. Powerful players usually hit the most home runs.

roster – This is a list of the players on the team.

stolen base – This is when a runner runs to the next base even though the ball has not been hit. Fast players usually steal the most bases.

umpire – This person makes sure both teams follow the rules and the game is played fairly.

Source 2

Ken helped coach the Oak City Acorns. He was an assistant manager. The Acorns were about to play a big game. They needed a victory. But where was the manager? Charles never missed a game.

Ken listened to a message on his cell phone. It was from Charles.

"Sorry, Ken. I am really sick. Please coach the team to victory. The first thing you need to do is set the batting order. A good batting order is very important. Good luck!"

Ken began to think. What batting order would Charles choose? He knew that Charles always puts the catcher eighth and the pitcher ninth in the batting order. He knew that Charles always puts his fastest player first in the batting order and his most powerful player fourth in the batting order. The person with the highest batting average always bats third in the order. Ken remembered that the player who wears #7 on his uniform always bats seventh. The player who wears #13 bats second. He knew that a boy named Gabe always bats fifth.

Now Ken knew the correct order. He wrote the batting order on a card. He handed the card to the umpire.

Source 3

Oak City Acorns
Team Roster

Name	Uniform Number	Position	Batting Average	Home Runs	Stolen Bases
Ben	13	2B	.356	5	12
Eddie	29	CF	.345	3	77
Gabe	1	3B	.314	14	11
Henry	42	1B	.300	25	0
Jeff	18	P	.250	2	1
Jose	7	SS	.333	3	20
Phil	12	LF	.311	10	9
Sam	34	RF	.399	9	13
Todd	5	C	.303	6	4

The Batting Order (cont.)

Name: _____

Part 1: Use Source 3 to answer these questions. Write the correct symbol on each line. Write **>** (greater than), **<** (less than), or **=** (equal to).

1. home runs by Phil   _____   home runs by Gabe

2. stolen bases by Ben   _____   stolen bases by Phil

3. stolen bases by Phil   _____   home runs by Sam

Part 2: Fill in the bubble next to the best answer to each question.

4. Who is the pitcher for the Oak City Acorns?

   Ⓐ Ken   Ⓒ Todd

   Ⓑ Charles   Ⓓ Jeff

5. What is another word for *assistant* as it is used in Source 2?

   Ⓐ manager   Ⓒ player

   Ⓑ helper   Ⓓ umpire

6. In what order are the players listed in Source 3?

   Ⓐ in the order in which they bat

   Ⓑ in order by their positions

   Ⓒ in alphabetical order

   Ⓓ from highest batting average to lowest

Part 3: Search <u>Source 3</u> of "The Batting Order" to find one example of the following:

7. the greatest number that is less than 100 _____

The Batting Order *(cont.)*

Name: _____

Part 4: Use the sources to answer the following questions.

8. Which of these players does not play an **infield** position? Circle the name and then explain your answer.

Jose   **Henry**   **Sam**

_____

_____

9. Complete the graph below.

▶ Write the names of the three teammates who play the outfield positions.

▶ Color in a baseball for each home run each player has hit.

Player Name	Position	Number of Home Runs
	LF	⚾ ⚾ ⚾ ⚾ ⚾ ⚾ ⚾ ⚾ ⚾ ⚾
	CF	⚾ ⚾ ⚾ ⚾ ⚾ ⚾ ⚾ ⚾ ⚾ ⚾
	RF	⚾ ⚾ ⚾ ⚾ ⚾ ⚾ ⚾ ⚾ ⚾ ⚾

The Batting Order (cont.)

Name: _____

10. What did the final lineup card look like? Fill out the lineup card for Ken. Use all of the clues given in Sources 2 and 3. For each player, write the name, uniform number, and position. Some information has been written in for you.

 Oak City Acorns
Batting Order

ORDER	PLAYER NAME	UNIFORM NUMBER	POSITION
1		29	
2	Ben		
3			RF
4		42	
5			
6	Phil		LF
7		7	
8	Todd		
9			

Unit 21

Gone the Way Of

Read each source below and on page 91. Then complete the activities on pages 92–94.

Source 1

Beth held an old book in her hand. "Look, Grandma. I found this in that box in your closet."

"Oh dear!" exclaimed Grandma. "I haven't seen one of these in years. That is one of *my* grandmother's diaries. Her name was Elizabeth, just like yours. When she was a child, she filled up a lot of diaries with her thoughts."

"Your grandmother? So that would make her my great-great-grandmother?"

"That's correct," said Grandma. "Let's see. This diary is from 1909. She kept a diary for almost every year she lived. She wrote all of those diaries by hand. I used to read these when I was a little girl. Her handwriting brings back a lot of memories for me."

"Wow," said Beth. "That's a lot of handwriting. I'm glad I can just text my thoughts or type them up on my computer. It's so much quicker."

"Yes," nodded Grandma. "Unfortunately, handwriting has gone the way of the Tin Lizzie."

"What? What does that mean?"

"It's an old saying. You say that about something that used to be popular but is not anymore."

Beth laughed, "Grandma, I think that saying has gone the way of the Tin Lizzie!"

Source 2

Blast from the Past! The Ford Model T

▲ This automobile was produced from October 1908 to May 1927.

▲ It was the first car that many families could afford to buy.

▲ It was the most popular automobile of its time.

▲ It was often called "Tin Lizard" or "Tin Lizzie."

Source 3

January 1, 1909

It is another year. This will be the second year that I have kept a diary. I hope I keep one for the rest of my life.

So many things happened last year. My little sister was born. I started school. Our dog had puppies. I wonder what this year will bring.

As always,
Elizabeth

Source 4

January 9, 1909

We finally bought a Model T! It seems like everyone but us had one. Mother says that's not true. I know she is right.

Father says it cost a lot of money but it will make our lives better. He also said we could take trips to the lake now. It will only take an hour to get there. The lake is almost 20 miles away!

As ever,
Elizabeth

Name: _____

Part 1: Read each idea. Which source gives you this information? Fill in the correct bubble for each source. (Note: More than one bubble may be filled in for each idea.)

Information	Sources ➡	1	2	3	4
1. A girl named Elizabeth kept a diary.		○	○	○	○
2. Elizabeth's family bought a Model T in 1909.		○	○	○	○
3. The Model T was very popular in 1909.		○	○	○	○

Part 2: Fill in the bubble next to the best answer to each question.

4. Sources 3 and 4 look like pages from a _____.

    Ⓐ diary   Ⓒ newspaper

    Ⓑ calendar   Ⓓ dictionary

5. The "Lizzie" in "Tin Lizzie" is short for which word?

    Ⓐ Beth   Ⓒ Lizard

    Ⓑ Elizabeth   Ⓓ both A and B

6. Which of these things did **not** happen in 1908?

    Ⓐ The Model T was first produced.

    Ⓑ Beth's grandma was born.

    Ⓒ Elizabeth started school.

    Ⓓ Elizabeth started keeping a diary.

Part 3: Search <u>Source 2</u> of "Gone the Way Of" to find one example of the following:

7. a word that **begins and ends** with a vowel _____

Name: _____

Part 4: Use the sources to answer the following questions.

8. How long after the Model T was first produced did Elizabeth's family buy one? Circle the correct answer. Then explain how you found this answer.

about three months   **almost one year**   **over two years**

_____

_____

_____

_____

9. How does Beth's grandmother feel about handwriting "going the way of the Tin Lizzie"? How do you know this from the story?

_____

_____

_____

_____

_____

_____

_____

Name: _____

Part 4 *(cont.)*: Use the sources to answer these questions.

10. Think about an object that is very popular right now. Write at least three things about the object. Pretend that you are describing it to someone who is alive over 100 years from now and who has never seen or used this object before.

Blast from the Past!

_____
Name of the Object

A Picture of the Object

_____

_____

_____

_____

_____

_____

_____

_____

_____

_____

Making Water Move

Read each source below and on page 96. Then complete the activities on pages 97–99.

Source 1

WHO AND WHAT?

Aesop — Aesop was a Greek storyteller who lived over 2,500 years ago. He is *credited* with writing a collection of fables. (This means that we think he wrote them, but we don't know for certain.)

Fable — Fables are short stories written to teach lessons. The characters in fables are often animals who act more like people.

Source 2

The Crow and the Pitcher
a retelling of an Aesop's fable

A very thirsty crow came upon a pitcher that contained some water. He knew he needed water to stay alive. But when the crow put its beak into the mouth of the pitcher, he found that he could not reach far enough down into it. His beak was not long enough, and the pitcher was too deep. The water was beyond his reach. He tried, and he tried, but at last had to give up. Then a thought came to him. He took a pebble and dropped it into the pitcher. Then he took another pebble and dropped it into the pitcher. He did this many times. The water rose up inside the container. At last, he was able to reach the water with his beak. With great relief, he drank from the pitcher. The water saved his life.

Mr. Pine was teaching a science experiment. He had a glass bowl. The bowl was filled halfway with water. He also had a toy boat made of plastic.

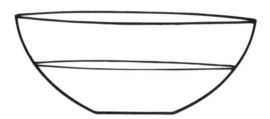 

Mr. Pine said, "Class, let's see what happens when we put the boat into the water."

He placed the boat in the water. The water level rose. It came up. The boat floated near the top of the water.

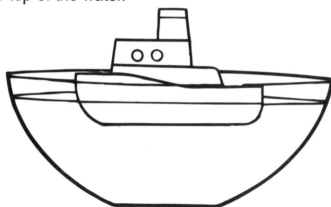

"We can observe a few things. First, we see that the bottom of the boat sinks into the water a little bit. Most of the boat stays above the water. The force of the water pushes up on the boat. The weight of the boat pushes down on the water. These two weights are just about equal. That is why the boat floats."

"We can also see the water level rise inside the bowl. Why does it do that? The weight of the boat **displaces** some of the water. To displace something is to force it to move somewhere. The solid boat forces the liquid water to move out of its way. The water has to go somewhere. The water moves from down there to up here."

Making Water Move *(cont.)*

Name: _____

Part 1: Read each idea. Which source gives you this information? Fill in the correct bubble for each source. (Note: More than one bubble may be filled in for each idea.)

Information	Sources ➡	1	2	3
1. Mr. Pine teaches science.		○	○	○
2. Fables are short stories.		○	○	○
3. Most fables have animal characters.		○	○	○

Part 2: Fill in the bubble next to the best answer to each question.

4. In the fable, a pebble is a small _____ and a pitcher is a large _____.

 Ⓐ rock, baseball player   Ⓒ container, rock

 Ⓑ rock, container   Ⓓ crow, beak

5. Why was it important for Mr. Pine to use a glass bowl for his experiment?

 Ⓐ so the boat would float better   Ⓒ so the bowl would be wider

 Ⓑ so the water would rise more   Ⓓ so the class could see the water

6. In Source 1, it says that Aesop is "credited" with writing many fables. Which phrase from Source 1 most likely tells you why we don't know for certain if he wrote them?

 Ⓐ "Aesop was a Greek storyteller"

 Ⓑ "who lived over 2,500 years ago"

 Ⓒ "Fables are short stories"

 Ⓓ "The characters in fables are often animals"

Part 3: Search <u>Source 3</u> of "Making Water Move" to find the following:

7. a word that rhymes with "great" _____

Name: _____

Part 4: Use the sources to answer the following questions.

8. Draw two pictures to illustrate the fable "The Crow and the Pitcher."

In picture 1 . . .

Show a glass pitcher with water in it. Show the crow trying to drink the water and not being able to reach it.

In picture 2 . . .

Show what the pitcher looks like at the end of the fable. Show the crow drinking the water.

Making Water Move (cont.)

Name: _____

Part 4 (cont.): Use the sources to answer these questions.

9. Look at the container in Source 3. Would the crow have had an easier time getting water out of that container? Why or why not?

_____

_____

_____

_____

10. How does the fable relate to Mr. Pine's science experiment? How does the crow use the same ideas Mr. Pine teaches to get water to drink?

_____

_____

_____

_____

_____

_____

_____

_____

1. Now that you have read all of the sources for this unit, do you see any connections between them? What do they have in common? Find at least one connection.

_____

_____

2. Fill in the chart below to show the elements that describe each source. You may fill in as many bubbles as are appropriate. (Note: Some rows will be left blank if there are fewer than four sources in the unit.)

Source # Element ➡	fiction	nonfiction	chart or graph	map or diagram
Source 1	○	○	○	○
Source 2	○	○	○	○
Source 3	○	○	○	○
Source 4	○	○	○	○

3. It's your turn to be a teacher. Write a new multiple-choice question based on the reading sources. Then provide two answer choices, only one of which is correct.

Your Question: _____

_____

Ⓐ _____

Ⓑ _____

4. Once again, imagine that you are the teacher. Think of one word, phrase, number, etc., that your students will need to search the sources to find. For example, give the definition of a word, and have everyone find that word. Challenge your "students" to find a word with a certain number of syllables. There are many possibilities.

Search for _____

Answer Key

Unit 1. Primary Colors (page 6)

Part 1
1. Source 1
2. Source 3
3. Source 3

Part 2
4. A
5. B
6. B

Part 3
7. schooling

Part 4
8.

Top Light	Middle Light	Bottom Light
Line 1: red	Line 1: yellow	Line 1: green
Line 2: primary	Line 2: primary	Line 2: secondary
Line 3: stop	Line 3: caution	Line 3: go

9. *In the box:* "3. not made from or caused by anything else"
On the lines: Accept appropriate responses. Students may say this definition fits because the three primary colors are not made from anything else. They can be mixed together to make other colors, but other colors cannot be mixed together to make them.

10. Accept appropriate answers. Students may say that it was a good idea to add a yellow light. This is especially true for today's drivers. Most listen to music or talk on the phone, and so they would not be able to hear a buzzer.

Unit 2. Buzz Words (page 10)

Part 1
1. Sources 1 and 3
2. Sources 1, 2, and 3
3. Source 3

Part 2
4. A
5. B
6. D

Part 3
7. enemies

Part 4
8. She should wear white or another light color. Bees are more likely to attack someone wearing dark colors because their enemies are dark-colored. If a bee thinks you are an enemy, it might sting you.

9. The arrow is pointing to the veil. "I wear a veil to protect my face and neck."

10. Circled words: whirred, chirped, squawked

Unit 3. Star Light, Star Bright (page 14)

Part 1
1. Source 2
2. Sources 1, 2, and 3
3. Sources 1 and 3

Part 2
4. C
5. D
6. C

Part 3
7. Earth

Part 4
8. A star would be more likely to look as though it is twinkling on a very windy day. That is because you would be looking at the light through a lot of moving air. Source 1 explains this.

9. Accept appropriate responses. Example: Tim's dad said, "Sirius is a part of Canis Major. It is the brightest star in Canis Major. In Latin, the words 'Canis Major' mean 'big dog.' Because Sirius is the brightest star in this constellation, it is often called the 'Dog Star.'"

10. A.

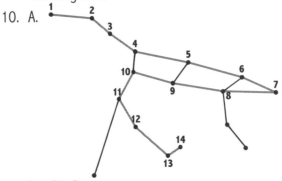

B. Big Bear
C. Accept appropriate responses.
D. Accept appropriate responses.

Answer Key *(cont.)*

Unit 4. Award-Winning Cookies *(page 18)*

Part 1
1. Sources 1 and 2
2. Sources 2 and 3
3. Source 2

Part 2
4. B
5. A
6. D

Part 3
7. prize

Part 4
8. The recipe calls for 24 tablespoons of sugar. In Source 1, the recipe tells us that $1\frac{1}{2}$ cups of sugar are needed. In Source 4, we learn that 8 tablespoons equal $\frac{1}{2}$ cup and 16 tablespoons equal one cup. $16 + 8 = 24$. That means that 24 tablespoons equal $1\frac{1}{2}$ cups.

9. Accept appropriate responses. The person in the picture should look unhappy or disgusted. The sentence should describe the person as not liking the taste and/or texture of the cookie.

10. Lily's cookies did not taste or look right because she used too much baking soda. The recipe in Source 1 calls for two <u>teaspoons</u> of baking soda. In Source 2, we learn that she used two <u>tablespoons</u> of baking soda. Based on the information in Source 4, two tablespoons would equal six teaspoons. That is three times as much baking soda as was needed.

Unit 5. Many Moons Ago *(page 22)*

Part 1
1. Sources 2 and 4
2. Source 2
3. Sources 1 and 4

Part 2
4. A
5. B
6. C

Part 3
7. natural

Part 4
8. There are eight **planets** in our solar system. Combined, there are over 170 **moons** in our solar system. Many **planets** have two or more **moons**. Mercury and Venus do not have any **moons**.

   Many **moons** ago, we knew less about our solar system. With new telescopes and spacecraft, we learn more and more all of the time.

9. The planet must have been Saturn. From 2004 to 2014, Saturn is the only planet around which we discovered that many moons.

10. A chart from 2024 might show that there are even more moons in our solar system. We may develop new telescopes or spacecraft that allow us to discover moons that are there but haven't been found yet.

Unit 6. Supply the Answer *(page 26)*

Part 1
1. Sources 1, 2, and 3
2. Sources 2 and 3
3. Sources 1 and 2

Part 2
4. B
5. C
6. B

Part 3
7. metal

Part 4
8. 1. Turn left onto Apple Ln. 2. Turn right onto Orange Ave. 3. Turn right onto Peach St. 4. Turn right onto Lime St. 5. Turn left onto Cherry Way. 6. Turn left onto Lemon St. Office World is on the right.

9. She will pay him $75. She will give him $70 to pay him back for what he spent at Office World. She will give him $5 for gas money. Together, these amounts equal $75.

10. Accept appropriate responses. In short messages, students should nicely point out to Trevor that he forgot to buy a box of pencils.

Answer Key *(cont.)*

Unit 7. An Insect Emerges (page 31)

Part 1

1. Sources 1 and 4
2. Source 3
3. Source 4

Part 2

4. A
5. B
6. A

Part 3

7. hat

Part 4

8. A. Students should add two antennae to the head, six legs to the thorax, and an abdomen at the back of the insect. B. Students should add the word *egg* below the first drawing. For the second stage, they should draw a caterpillar. For the fourth, they should draw a butterfly.
9. Spiders are different from insects in several ways. Students can reference Sources 1 and 3 to explain those differences. Spiders have two main body parts, while insects have three. Spiders have eight legs, while insects have six. Spiders have palps, while insects have antennae.
10. Accept appropriate answers.

Unit 8. Stop and Go (page 36)

Part 1

1. halted, traffic
2. blocked, cars
3. cease, noise

Part 2

4. C
5. A

Part 3

6. our
7. idea

Part 4

8. In the beginning, the narrator is enjoying a quiet day. In the middle, a traffic jam causes a loud noise on the street below the narrator's window. In the end, the traffic jam clears up, and the noise goes away.

9. Accept appropriate responses.
10. Accept appropriate responses. Students should use a different synonym to replace each of the seven underlined words and phrases in Source 3.

Unit 9. Sign Language (page 40)

Part 1

1. Sources 2 and 3
2. Source 3
3. Source 3

Part 2

4. C
5. D
6. B

Part 3

7. circle

Part 4

8. The stop sign should be crossed out. Order of other signs: School sign (3), Railroad (4), Yield (1), Deer Crossing (2)
9. Accept appropriate answers. Students should choose a sign from Source 2 that is not mentioned in Source 3. Students should have Tess ask a question based on the shape of the sign or its color (if students know this information). They should answer the question with information about the meaning of the sign.
10. Accept appropriate responses. Students may say that as a narrator, Tess would be excited to learn more about the world around her. She might be impatient with her mother or brother's answers, or she might be grateful that they take the time to answer all of her questions.

Unit 10. The Fast and the Slow (page 44)

Part 1

1. Sources 1 and 2
2. Sources 1 and 3
3. Sources 3 and 4

Part 2

4. B
5. A
6. D

Answer Key *(cont.)*

Part 3

7. clinging

Part 4

8. Students should circle "snail." In Source 3, we learn that the snail is the world's slowest animal on land. Therefore, a unit titled "The Fastest and the Slowest" should probably be about cheetahs and snails.

9. Accept appropriate responses. Students can give many differences between the two animals (speed, habitats, diet, etc.). Cheetahs and sloths are similar in that they are both perfectly suited for their habitats. Also, each have special claws that are useful for their types of living.

10. Accept appropriate responses.

Unit 11. An Ancient Puzzle *(page 48)*

Part 1

1. Sources 1 and 4
2. Sources 3 and 4
3. Source 3

Part 2

4. C
5. D
6. A

Part 3

7. China

Part 4

8. Shape numbers may vary slightly.

   A. dog, animal

   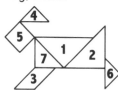

   B. sailboat, object

   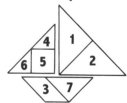

C. kangaroo, animal

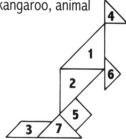

Part 5

9. Accept appropriate responses.

10. Accept appropriate attempts to form an object or animal from the seven pieces of the tangram.

Unit 12. Getting Enough Sleep *(page 52)*

Part 1

1. >
2. =
3. <

Part 2

4. B
5. A
6. B

Part 3

7. quieter

Part 4

8. Grace slept 16 total hours. According to the graph in Source 1, this is the amount a newborn baby should be getting.

9. Students should circle the choice, "We need more sleep when we are younger." Accept appropriate responses as to why this may be true.

10. Accept appropriate responses.

Unit 13. The Baker's Dozen *(page 56)*

Part 1

1. Source 1
2. Source 3
3. Source 1

Part 2

4. C
5. B
6. A

Part 3

7. box

Part 4

8. Source 3 takes place on a Saturday. We know that Source 1 and Source 3 tell the same event from two different points of view. We know that Source 1 happens on a Saturday morning. That means that Source 3 happens on a Saturday morning, too.

9. She will probably notice. She has been buying boxes of donuts at this donut shop for a long time. The man in Source 3 says that his shop has always given customers a free donut when they buy a dozen.

10. Students should draw 10 more donuts inside the box. Five of the donuts should have frosting. Four should have sprinkles. One should be a bar with stripes. The three cinnamon rolls are already drawn inside the box.

Unit 14. Extra Extra! *(page 60)*

Part 1

1. Sources 1 and 3
2. Source 2
3. Source 3

Part 2

4. A
5. B
6. C

Part 3

7. complicated

Part 4

8. A.

Cheese	Mushroom	Pepperoni
IIII	II	NNI

   B. Yes, there will be one piece left over for her.

   C. The following should be drawn on the pizza: pepperoni pieces on 5 slices and mushroom pieces on 3 slices. Four slices should be left blank.

9. The pizza will cost $24. In Source 1, the pizza is advertised as costing $20. The caption tells us that each additional topping will cost $2. There are two extra toppings to be added—pepperoni and mushrooms. That adds $4 onto the cost of the pizza. $20 + $4 = $24.

10. A. Extranormous
    B. extra and enormous
    C. Accept appropriate responses.
    D. Accept appropriate responses.

Unit 15. Show Their Stripes *(page 64)*

Part 1

1. Source 2
2. Source 1
3. Source 3

Part 2

4. D
5. C
6. A

Part 3

7. meat

Part 4

8. Zebras use the tall grass to hide from predators. Grass is the main food that zebras eat.

9. Same: both have black and white stripes; Different: Each zebra has a different stripe pattern, while referees all wear the same vertical pattern. Also, zebras use their stripes to blend into their environment. Referees use their stripes to stand out from the other people on the field (the players).

10. Students should draw thick vertical stripes (black and white) on the shirt. Students should draw five horizontal stripes (blue) on the fish. These stripes should go from the fish's head to its tail.

Unit 16. Sharing a Name *(page 68)*

Part 1

1. Source 3
2. Sources 2, 3, and 4
3. Sources 3 and 4

Part 2

4. C
5. B
6. D

Part 3

7. United States

Answer Key *(cont.)*

Part 4

8. They have different-color hair. One likes meat, while the other is a vegetarian. They come from different parts of the United States. The Kira from Ohio is older.

9. They are both from New Zealand. They are both brown on the outside.

10. We know that the kiwi bird (circled) was named first because the fruit was named after it. That happened in 1959. We know that Kira from New York (underlined) was named last because she was born one year after Kira from Ohio.

Unit 17. Write and Wrong (page 72)

Part 1

1. Rules 1 and 2
2. Rules 1, 4, and 5
3. Rules 1, 3, and 5

Part 2

4. B
5. D
6. A

Part 3

7. Capitalization

Part 4

8. Dear Danny,

    My trip is almost over. I can't wait to see you and Mom. I should fly back into the United <u>States</u> by <u>Halloween</u>. What costume will you wear this year<u>?</u>

    I talked to Mom about you yesterday. She <u>said</u> that you are becoming a very good reader and writer. I always <u>knew</u> you would <u>be</u> smart!

    Please <u>write</u> back to me when you get a chance. <u>I</u> would love to hear from you. This trip has been fun, but I miss my little brother<u>.</u>

    <u>See</u> you soon,
    Joey

9. Both words begin with a silent *w*.

10. Accept appropriate responses. Students should use one set of homophones, and those homophones should be underlined.

Unit 18. Useful Machines (page 76)

Part 1

1. four
2. March 5
3. Wednesday

Part 2

4. B
5. C
6. D

Part 3

7. squinted

Part 4

8. Source 3 takes place in the year 2021. The photo was taken in 1920, and Grandpa says that it is exactly 101 years old. 1920 + 101 = 2021.

9.

Type of Simple Machine	Name of Uncle	What It Is Helping Him Do
lever	Uncle Jack	to move a heavy rock
wedge	Uncle Bill	to split a tree trunk
wheel and axle	Uncle Rex	to move dirt and rocks
inclined plane	Uncle Rex	to move from one height to another

9. Uncle Jack, lever, to move a heavy rock; Uncle Bill, wedge, to split a tree trunk; Uncle Rex, wheel and axle and inclined plane, to move dirt and rocks from one place to another and up a ramp.

10. Accept appropriate responses that name a simple machine and tell one way it is used today.

Unit 19. Time Will Tell (page 80)

Part 1

1. Sources 3 and 4
2. Source 3
3. Sources 2 and 3

Part 2

4. C
5. A
6. B

Part 3

7. noon

Part 4

8. A. Lulu and Mom

   B. Lulu and her mother woke up in the middle of the night.

   C. This happened at about 2:10 a.m.

   D. The electricity went out.

9. The electricity went out throughout Lulu's neighborhood. We know this because she looked out her window. The streetlights were out, and there were no lights on in her neighbors' windows.

10. A.

   B. p.m.

   C.

   D. a.m.

   E. 3 hours, 15 minutes

Unit 20. The Batting Order *(page 85)*

Part 1

1. <

2. >

3. =

Part 2

4. D

5. B

6. C

Part 3

7. 77

Part 4

8. The name "Sam" should be circled. In Source 3, we are told that he plays "RF." In Source 1, we learn that "RF" stands for "right fielder" and that right fielder is an outfield position.

9.

Player Name	Position	Number of Home Runs
Phil	LF	⚾⚾⚾⚾⚾ ⚾⚾⚾⚾⚾
Eddie	CF	⚾⚾⚾⚪⚪ ⚪⚪⚪⚪⚪
Sam	RF	⚾⚾⚾⚾⚾ ⚾⚾⚾⚾⚪

10.

Order	Player Name	Uniform Number	Position
1	Eddie	29	CF
2	Ben	13	2B
3	Sam	34	RF
4	Henry	42	1B
5	Gabe	1	3B
6	Phil	12	LF
7	Jose	7	SS
8	Todd	5	C
9	Jeff	18	P

Answer Key *(cont.)*

Unit 21. Gone the Way Of *(page 90)*

Part 1

1. Sources 1, 3, and 4
2. Source 4
3. Sources 2 and 4

Part 2

4. A
5. C
6. B

Part 3

7. automobile

Part 4

8. The correct answer is "about three months." In Source 2, we learn that the Model T was first produced in October of 1908. In Source 4, we learn that Elizabeth's family bought a Model T in January of 1909. The amount of time between those two events was about three months.

9. It makes her sad. Seeing the old handwriting brings back memories for her. Also, she says that it's unfortunate that no one handwrites anymore.

10. Accept appropriate responses. Students should draw a picture of the object and also write three things about it.

Unit 22. Making Water Move *(page 95)*

Part 1

1. Source 3
2. Sources 1 and 2
3. Source 1

Part 2

4. B
5. D
6. B

Part 3

7. weight

Part 4

8. In the first picture, students should draw a glass pitcher with water at the bottom. The neck of the pitcher should be too narrow for thhe crow to get its beak down to the bottom. In the second picture, students should draw the same pitcher. This time, there should be small pebbles at the bottom of the pitcher, and the water level should have risen to where the crow can reach it with its beak.

9. The bowl in Source 3 would have been easier for the crow because it has a wide opening and it is shallow. The crow would not have had a problem reaching the bottom of the bowl with his beak.

10. The fable illustrates the concept of displacement. The crow uses the pebbles to displace the water. The pebbles move the water level up. This allows the crow to reach the water inside the pitcher.

Common Core State Standards

The lessons and activities included in *Mastering Complex Text Using Multiple Reading Sources, Grade 2* meet the following Common Core State Standards. (©Copyright 2010. National Governors Association Center for Best Practices and Council of Chief State School Officers. All rights reserved.) For more information about Common Core State Standards, go to *http://www.corestandards.org/* or visit *http://www.teachercreated.com/standards/* for more correlations to Common Core State Standards.

Reading: Informational Text	
Key Ideas and Details	**Units**
ELA.RI.2.1 Ask and answer such questions as *who, what, where, when, why*, and *how* to demonstrate understanding of key details in a text.	1–22
ELA.RI.2.2 Identify the main topic of a multiparagraph text as well as the focus of specific paragraphs within the text.	2, 3, 5, 7, 10, 12, 15–16, 18, 21–22
ELA.RI.2.3 Describe the connection between a series of historical events, scientific ideas or concepts, or steps in technical procedures in a text.	1–5, 7, 10, 12, 15–16, 18–19, 21–22
Craft and Structure	**Units**
ELA.RI.2.4 Determine the meaning of words and phrases in a text relevant to a *grade 2 topic or subject area.*	1–22
ELA.RI.2.5 Know and use various text features (e.g., captions, bold print, subheadings, glossaries, indexes, electronic menus, icons) to locate key facts or information in a text efficiently.	1–22
ELA.RI.2.6 Identify the main purpose of a text, including what the author wants to answer, explain, or describe.	1, 4–5, 10, 12, 14, 16–17, 21–22
Integration of Knowledge and Ideas	**Units**
ELA.RI.2.7 Explain how specific images (e.g., a diagram showing how a machine works) contribute to and clarify a text.	2–3, 7, 9–12, 15–16, 18–20, 22
ELA.RI.2.8 Describe how reasons support specific points the author makes in a text.	2–5, 7, 10, 12–13, 15–16, 19, 21–22
ELA.RI.2.9 Compare and contrast the most important points presented by two texts on the same topic.	4, 10, 15–16, 19, 21–22

Common Core State Standards *(cont.)*

Reading: Informational Text *(cont.)*	
Range of Reading and Level of Text Complexity	**Units**
ELA.RI.2.10 By the end of the year, read and comprehend informational texts, including history/social studies, science, and technical texts, in the grades 2–3 text complexity band proficiently, with scaffolding as needed at the high end of the range.	1–22

Reading: Literature	
Key Ideas and Details	**Units**
ELA.RL.2.1 Ask and answer such questions as *who, what, where, when, why*, and *how* to demonstrate understanding of key details in a text.	1–22
ELA.RL.2.2 Recount stories, including fables and folktales from diverse cultures, and determine their central message, lesson, or moral.	22
ELA.RL.2.3 Describe how characters in a story respond to major events and challenges.	9, 19, 22
Craft and Structure	**Units**
ELA.RL.2.5 Describe the overall structure of a story, including describing how the beginning introduces the story and the ending concludes the action.	8, 13, 16, 19, 22
ELA.RL.2.6 Acknowledge differences in the points of view of characters, including by speaking in a different voice for each character when reading dialogue aloud.	7, 9, 11–12, 19
Range of Reading and Level of Text Complexity	**Units**
ELA.RL.2.10 By the end of the year, read and comprehend literature, including stories and poetry, in the grades 2–3 text complexity band proficiently, with scaffolding as needed at the high end of the range.	1–22

Foundational Skills	
Phonics and Word Recognition	**Units**
ELA.RF.2.3 Know and apply grade-level phonics and word analysis skills in decoding words.	1–22
Fluency	**Units**
ELA.RF.2.4 Read with sufficient accuracy and fluency to support comprehension.	1–22

Common Core State Standards *(cont.)*

Writing	
Text Types and Purposes	**Units**
ELA.W.2.1 Write opinion pieces in which they introduce the topic or book they are writing about, state an opinion, supply reasons that support the opinion, use linking words (e.g., *because*, *and*, *also*) to connect opinion and reasons, and provide a concluding statement or section.	1, 3–4, 7–10, 13, 19, 21–22
ELA.W.2.2 Write informative/explanatory texts in which they introduce a topic, use facts and definitions to develop points, and provide a concluding statement or section.	1–22
ELA.W.2.3 Write narratives in which they recount a well-elaborated event or short sequence of events, include details to describe actions, thoughts, and feelings, use temporal words to signal event order, and provide a sense of closure.	3–4, 6, 9, 11–12, 17, 21
Research to Build and Present Knowledge	**Units**
ELA.W.2.7 Participate in shared research and writing projects (e.g., read a number of books on a single topic to produce a report; record science observations).	1–22
ELA.W.2.8 Recall information from experiences or gather information from provided sources to answer a question.	1–22

Language	
Conventions of Standard English	**Units**
ELA.L.2.1 Demonstrate command of the conventions of standard English grammar and usage when writing or speaking.	1–22
ELA.L.2.2 Demonstrate command of the conventions of standard English capitalization, punctuation, and spelling when writing.	1–22
ELA.L.2.2A Capitalize holidays, product names, and geographic names.	6, 11, 14, 16–17
Knowledge of Language	**Units**
ELA.L.2.3 Use knowledge of language and its conventions when writing, speaking, reading, or listening.	1–22

Common Core State Standards *(cont.)*

Language *(cont.)*	
Vocabulary Acquisition and Use	**Units**
ELA.L.2.4 Determine or clarify the meaning of unknown and multiple-meaning words and phrases based on grade 2 reading and content, choosing flexibly from an array of strategies.	1–22
ELA.L.2.4A Use sentence-level context as a clue to the meaning of a word or phrase.	1–22
ELA.L.2.4C Use a known root word as a clue to the meaning of an unknown word with the same root (e.g., *addition, additional*).	1–22
ELA.L.2.4E Use glossaries and beginning dictionaries, both print and digital, to determine or clarify the meaning of words and phrases.	1, 5, 8–11, 13, 17–20, 22
ELA.L.2.5 Demonstrate understanding of figurative language, word relationships, and nuances in word meanings.	1–22

Math: Number & Operations in Base Ten	
Understand place value.	**Units**
Math.2.NBT.A.4 Compare two three-digit numbers based on meanings of the hundreds, tens, and ones digits, using >, =, and < symbols to record the results of comparisons.	20

Math: Measurement and Data	
Work with time and money.	**Units**
Math.2.MD.C.7 Tell and write time from analog and digital clocks to the nearest five minutes, using *a.m.* and *p.m.*	13, 19
Represent and interpret data.	**Units**
Math.2.MD.D.10 Draw a picture graph and a bar graph (with single-unit scale) to represent a data set with up to four categories. Solve simple put-together, take-apart, and compare problems using information presented in a bar graph.	12

Math: Geometry	
Reason with shapes and their attributes.	**Units**
Math.2.G.A.1 Recognize and draw shapes having specified attributes, such as a given number of angles or a given number of equal faces. Identify triangles, quadrilaterals, pentagons, hexagons, and cubes.	9, 11